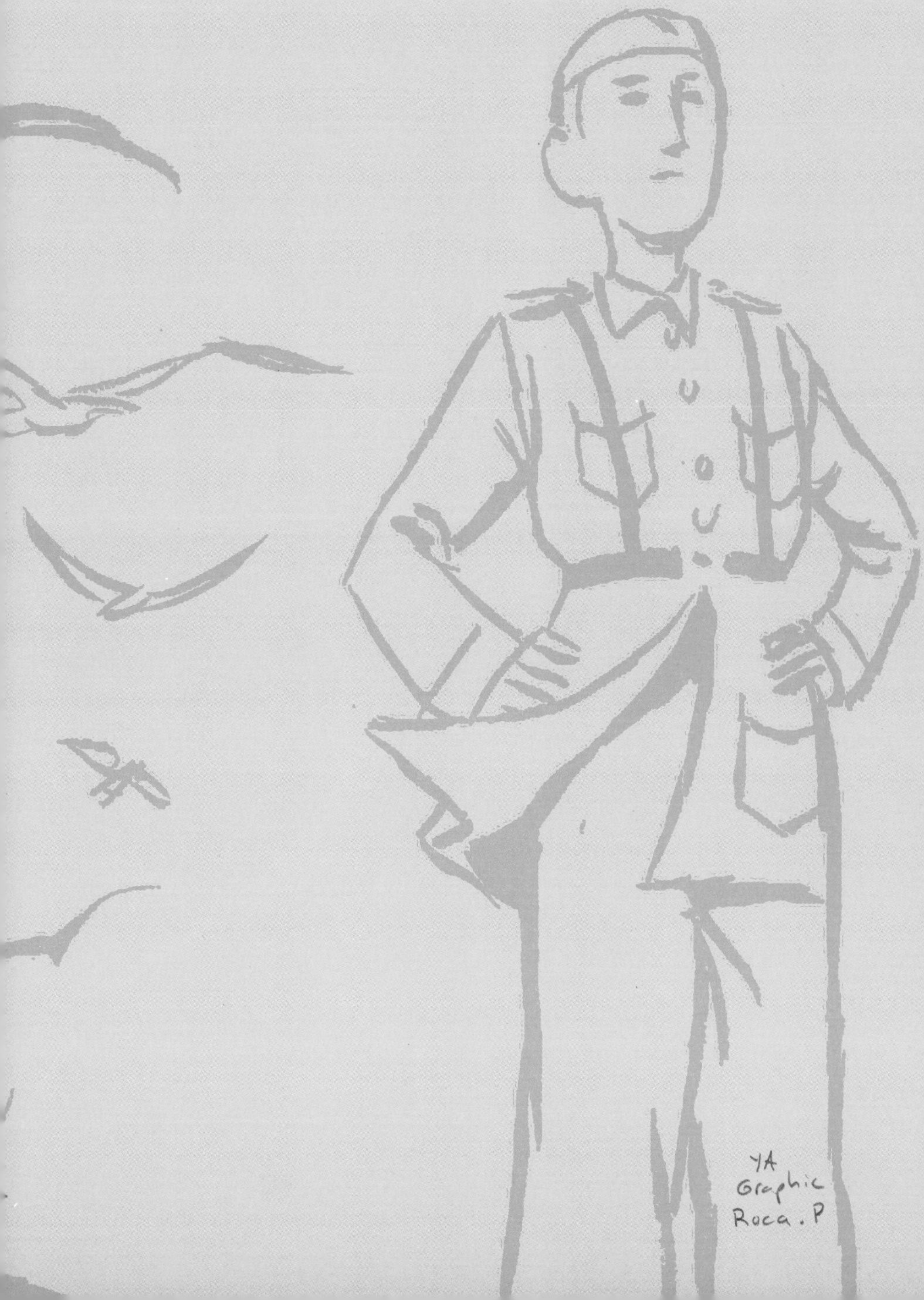

The Lighthouse

PACO ROCA

The Lighthouse

PACO ROCA

LIGHTHOUSE AT THE END OF THE WORLD J. VERNE
MOBY DICK
GULLIVER'S TRAVELS
TREASURE ISLAND
R.L. STEVENSON

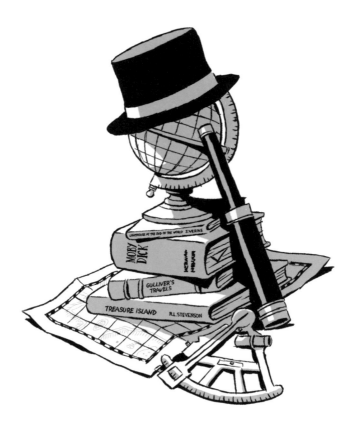

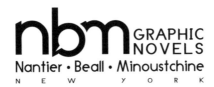

nbm GRAPHIC NOVELS
Nantier • Beall • Minoustchine
NEW YORK

ISBN 978-1-68112-056-0
Library of Congress Control Number: 2016917433
© 2004, 2009 Paco Roca
© 2014 Astiberri for the present edition
© 2017 NBM for the English translation
Translation by Jeff Whitman
Lettering by Ortho
Design by Manuel Bartual
Printed in China

1st printing February 2017
This book is also available wherever e-books are sold.

"Let the most absentminded of men be plunged
in his deepest reveries—stand that man on his
legs, set his feet a-going, and he will infallibly lead
you to water, if water there be in all that region."

Herman Melville, *Moby Dick*

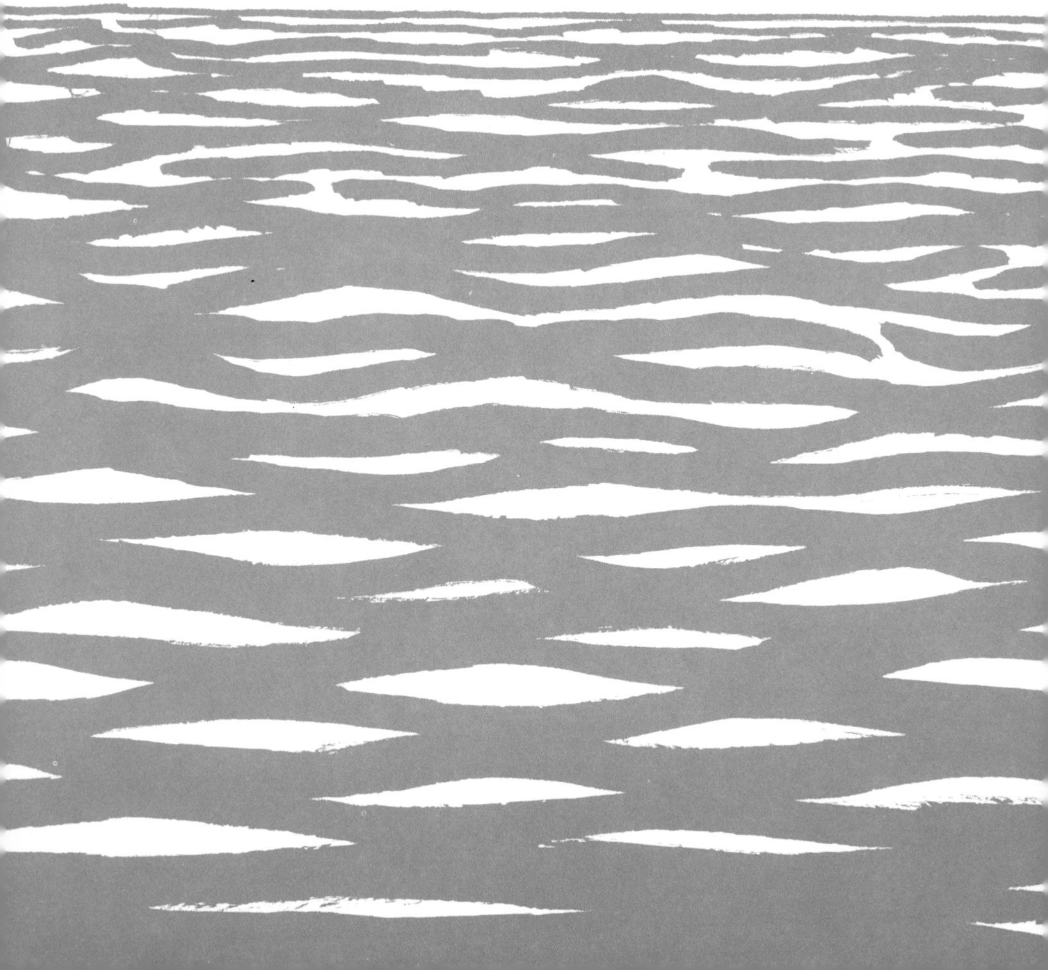

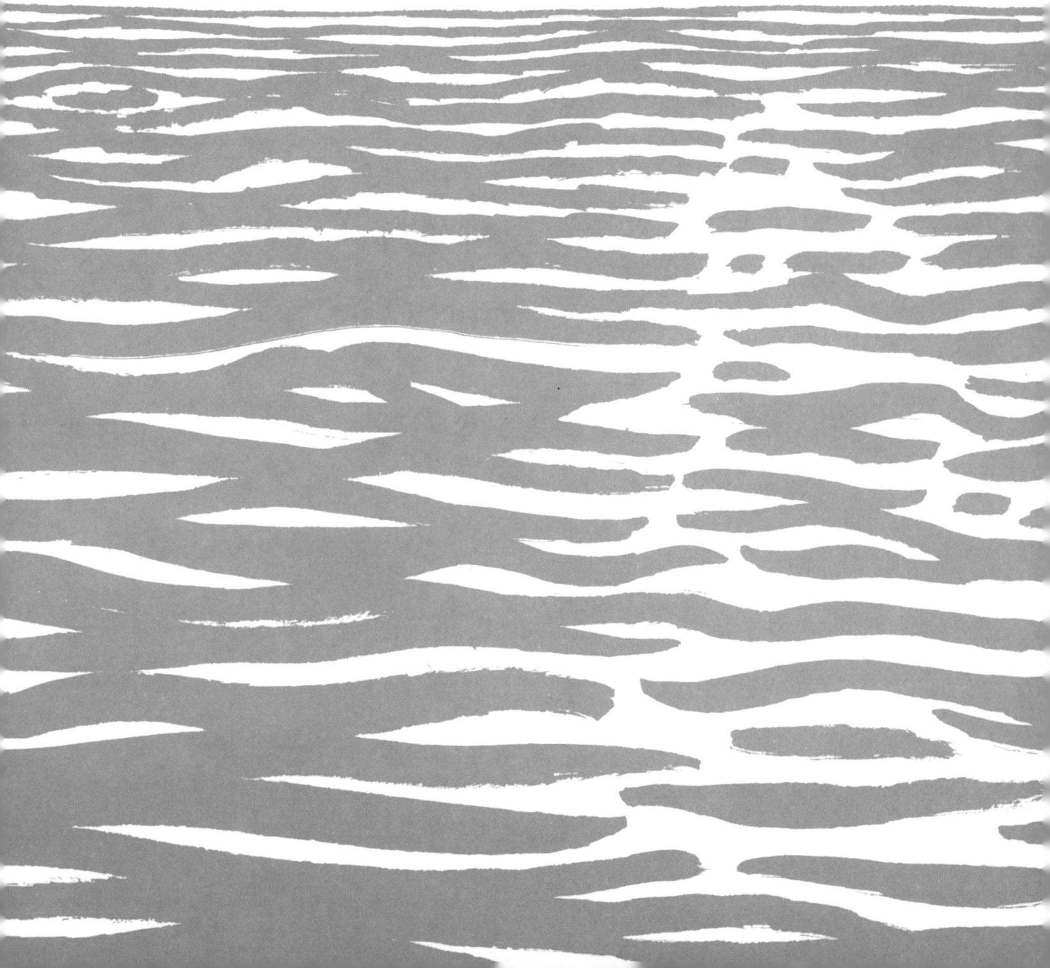

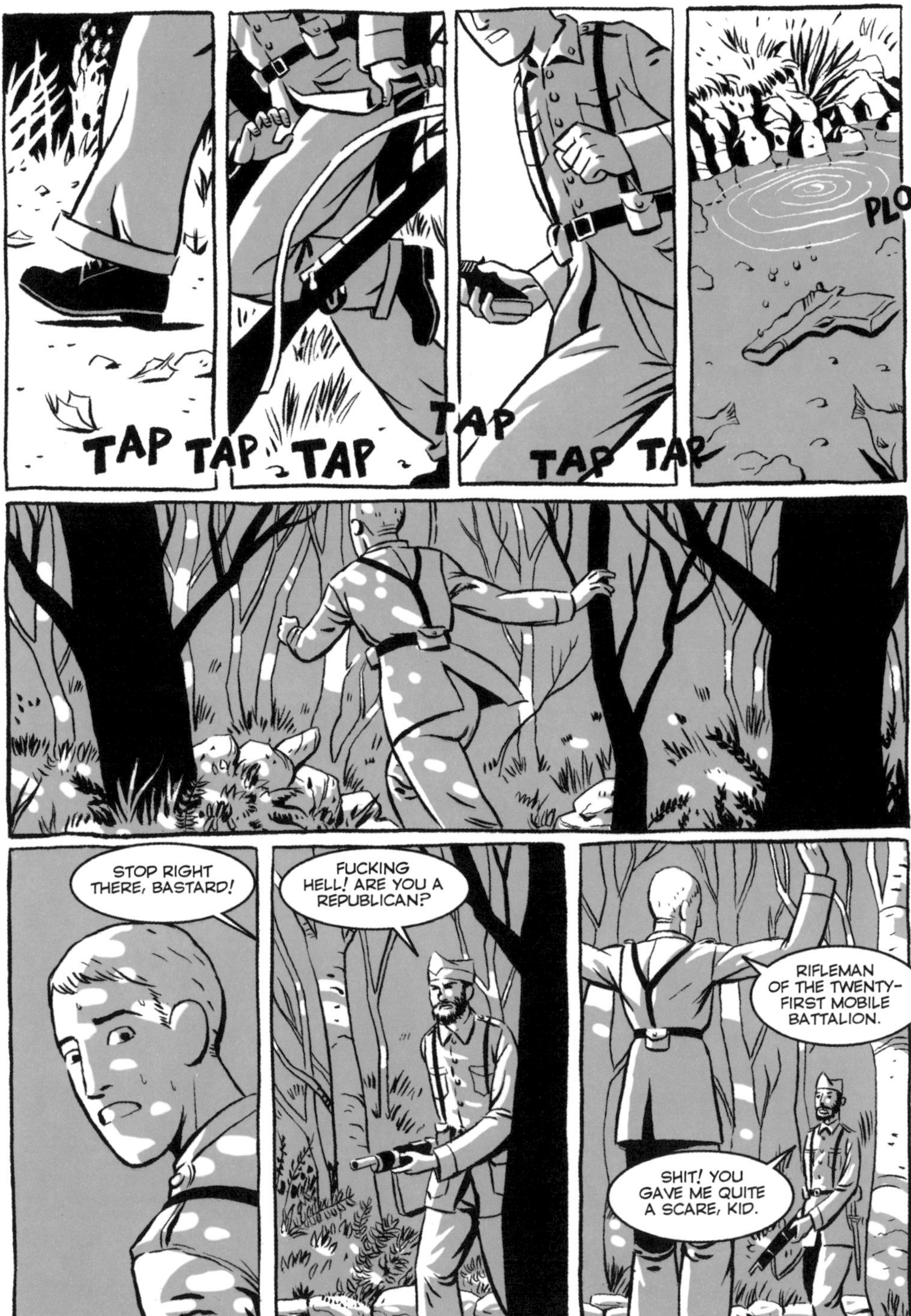
TAP TAP TAP
TAP
TAP TAP
PLOP
STOP RIGHT THERE, BASTARD!
FUCKING HELL! ARE YOU A REPUBLICAN?
RIFLEMAN OF THE TWENTY-FIRST MOBILE BATTALION.
SHIT! YOU GAVE ME QUITE A SCARE, KID.

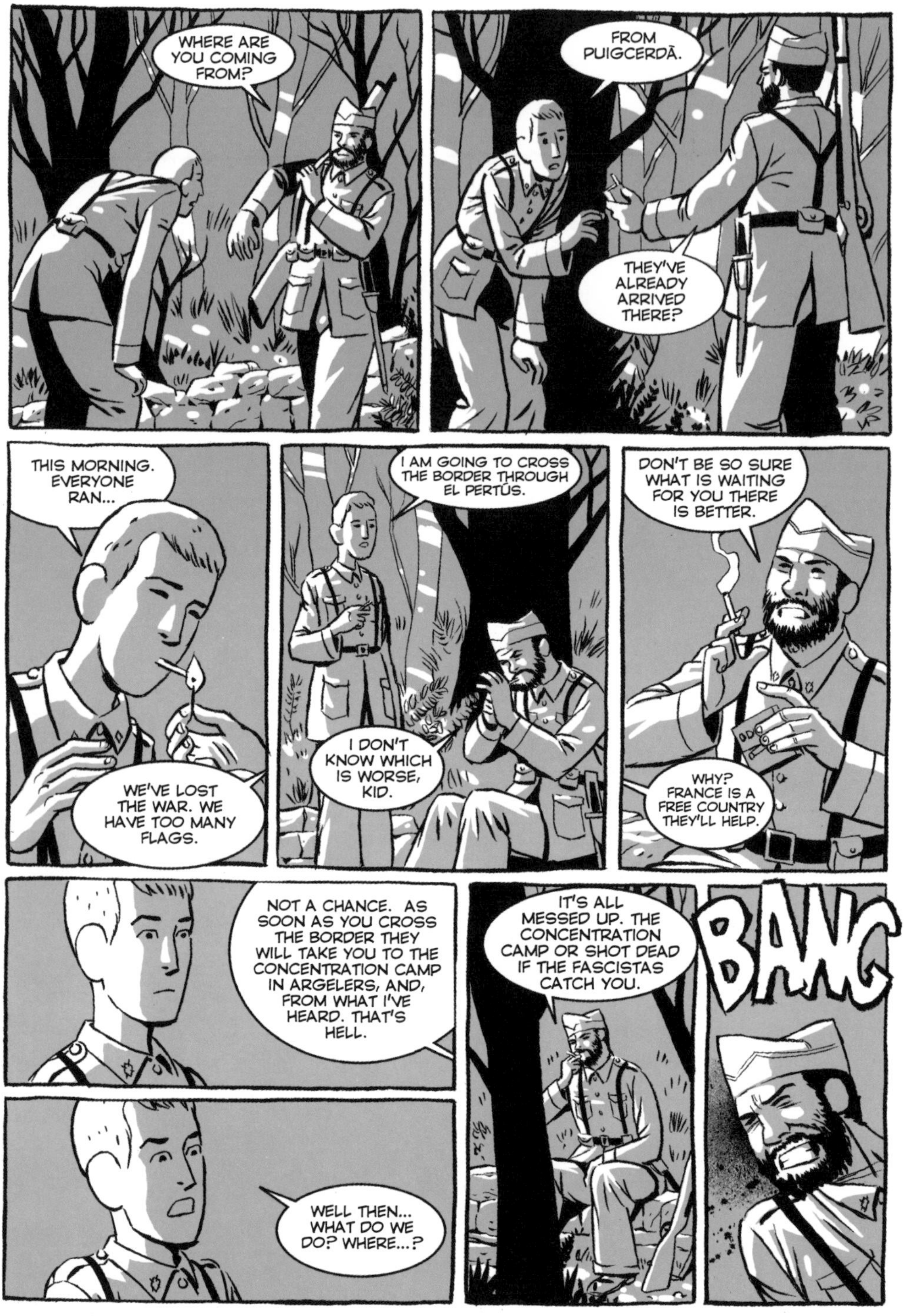
WHERE ARE YOU COMING FROM?
FROM PUIGCERDÃ.
THEY'VE ALREADY ARRIVED THERE?
THIS MORNING. EVERYONE RAN...
WE'VE LOST THE WAR. WE HAVE TOO MANY FLAGS.
I AM GOING TO CROSS THE BORDER THROUGH EL PERTÚS.
I DON'T KNOW WHICH IS WORSE, KID.
DON'T BE SO SURE WHAT IS WAITING FOR YOU THERE IS BETTER.
WHY? FRANCE IS A FREE COUNTRY THEY'LL HELP.
NOT A CHANCE. AS SOON AS YOU CROSS THE BORDER THEY WILL TAKE YOU TO THE CONCENTRATION CAMP IN ARGELERS, AND, FROM WHAT I'VE HEARD. THAT'S HELL.
WELL THEN... WHAT DO WE DO? WHERE...?
IT'S ALL MESSED UP. THE CONCENTRATION CAMP OR SHOT DEAD IF THE FASCISTAS CATCH YOU.
BANG

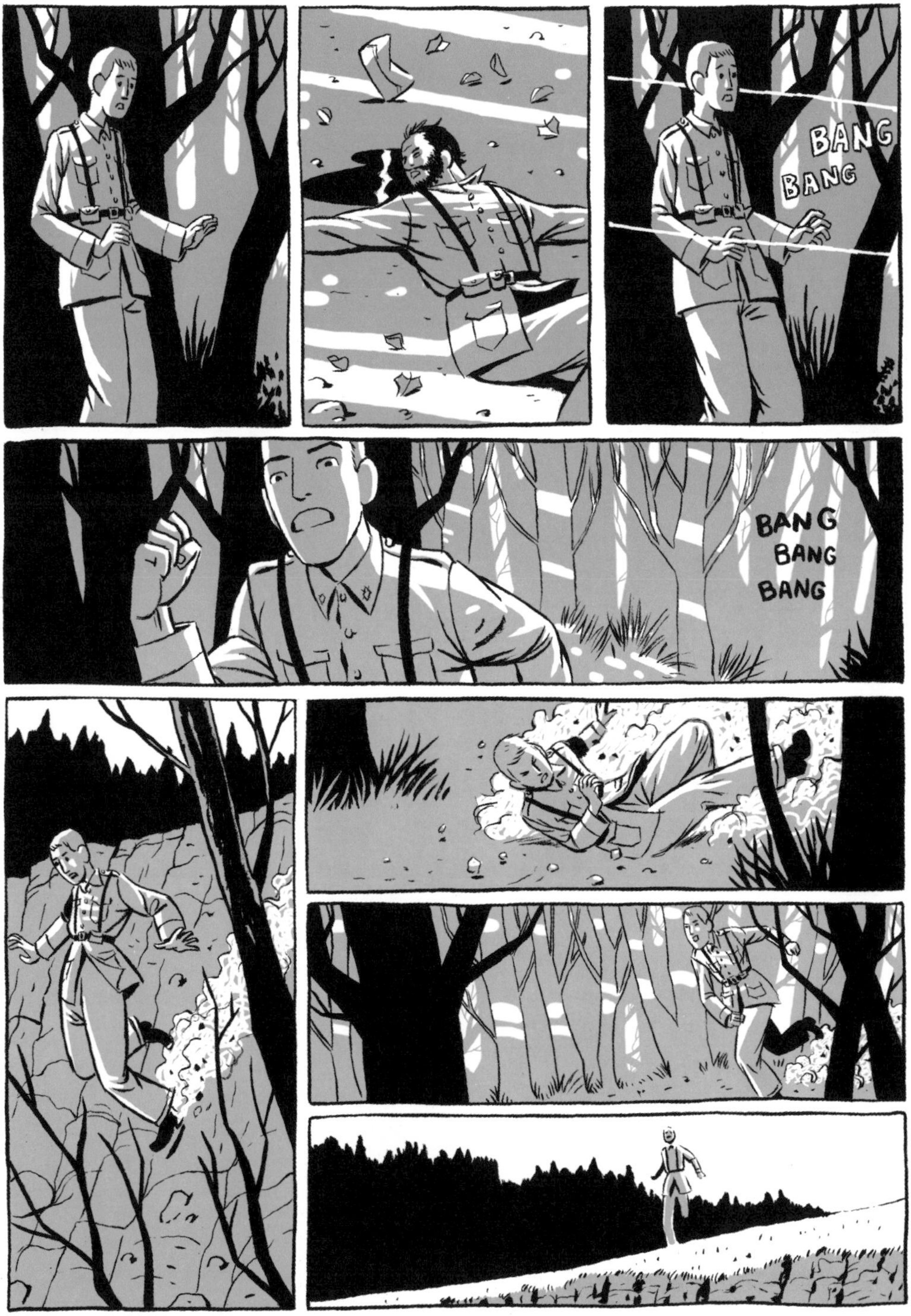
BANG
BANG
BANG
BANG
BANG

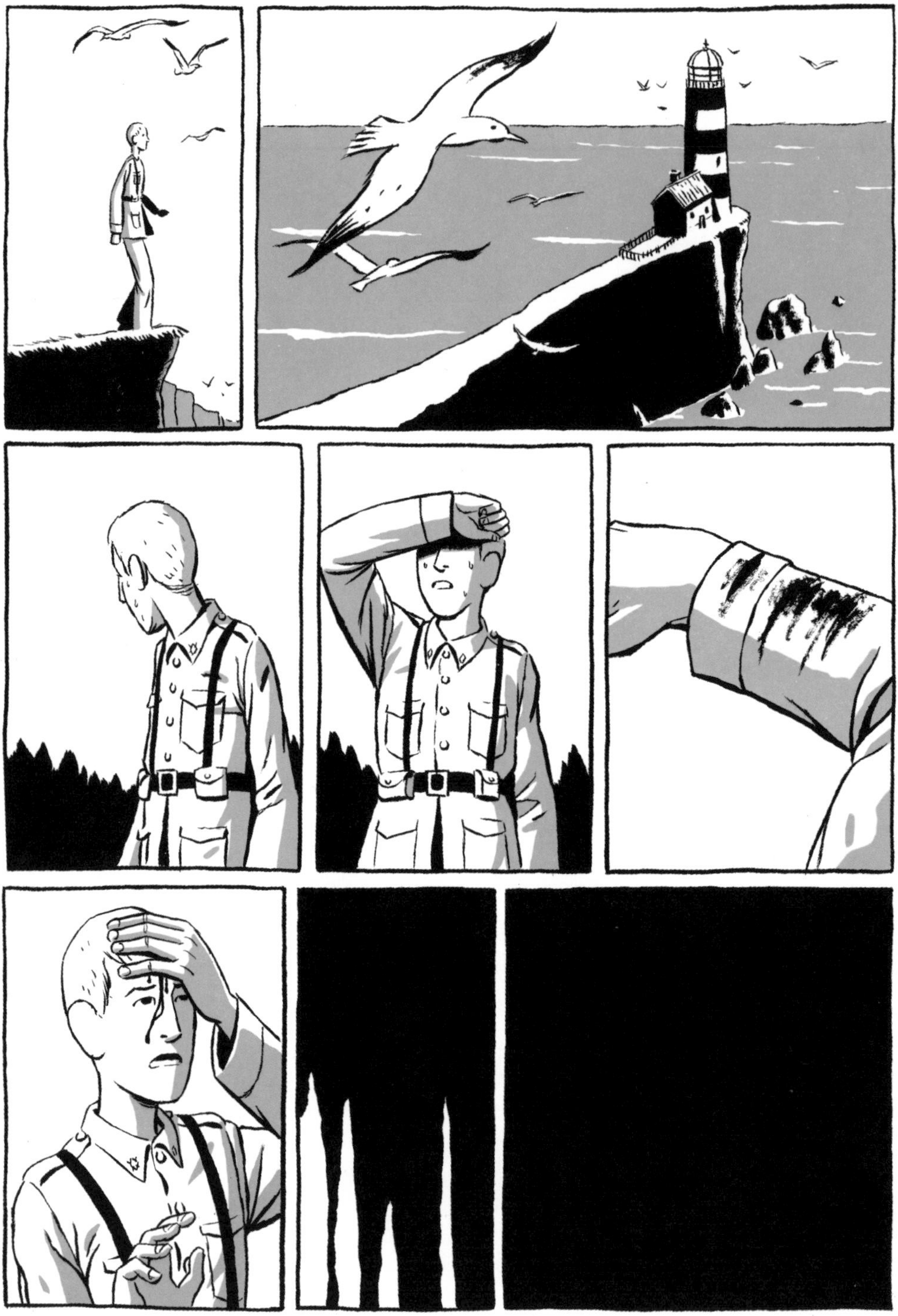

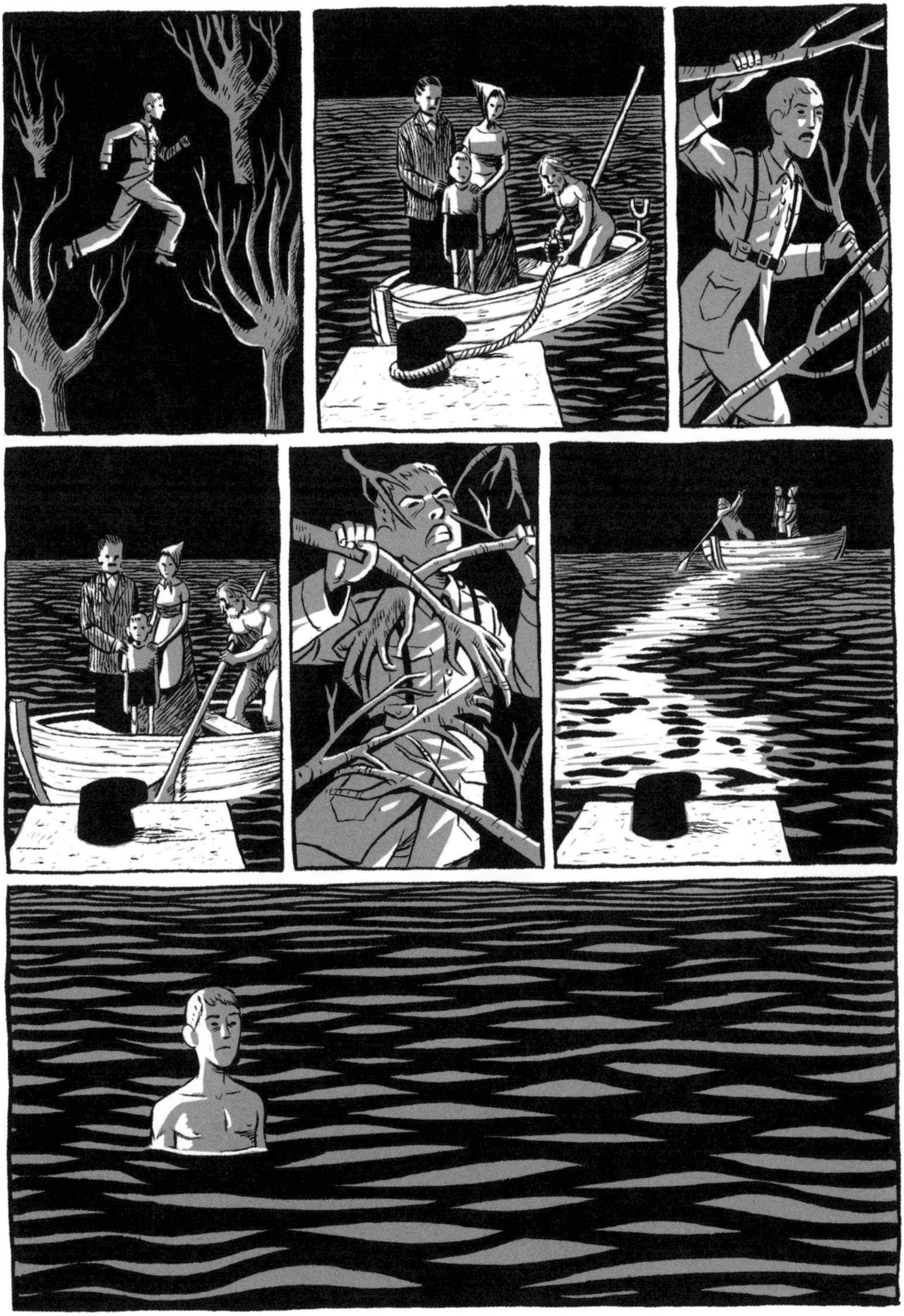

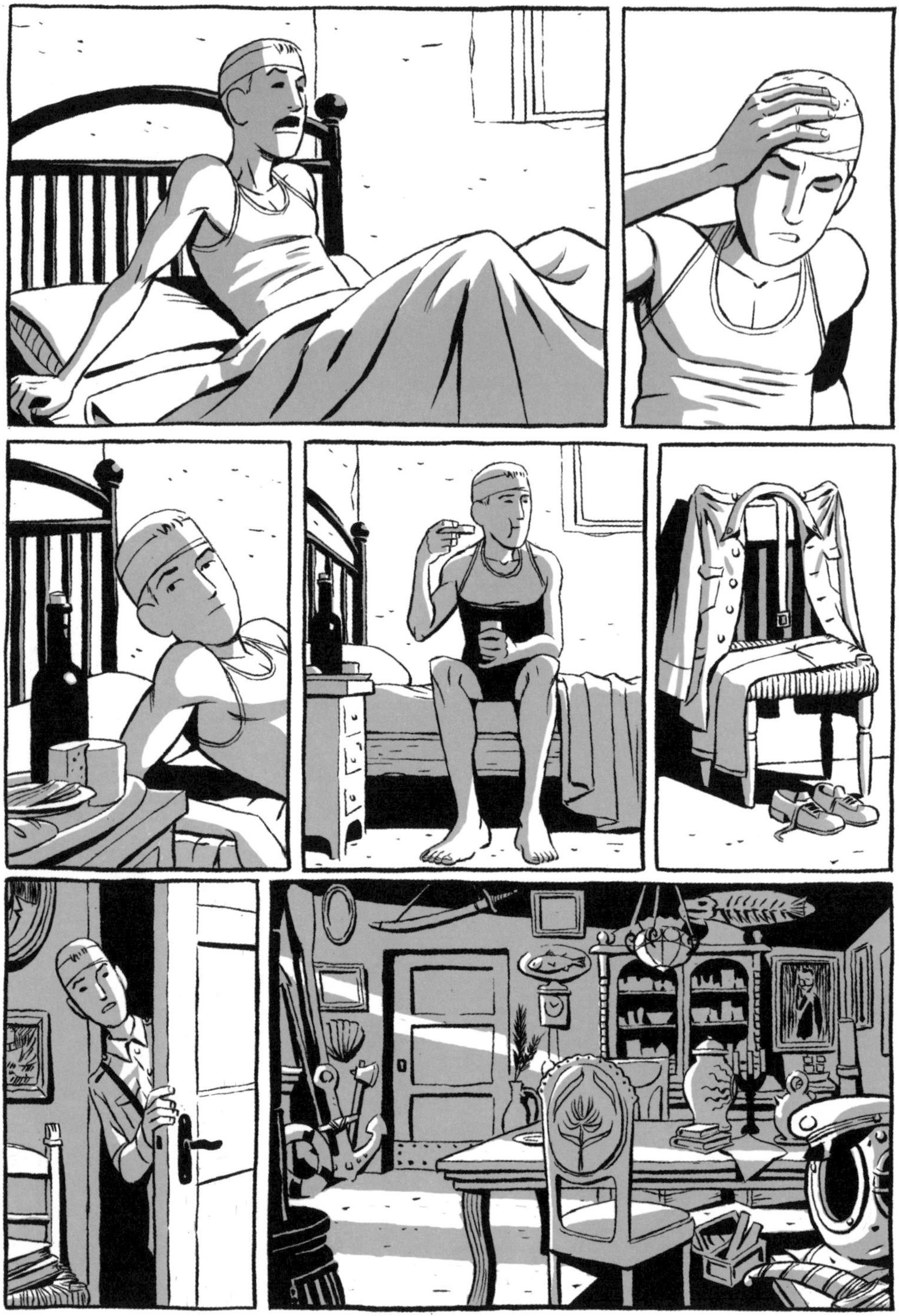

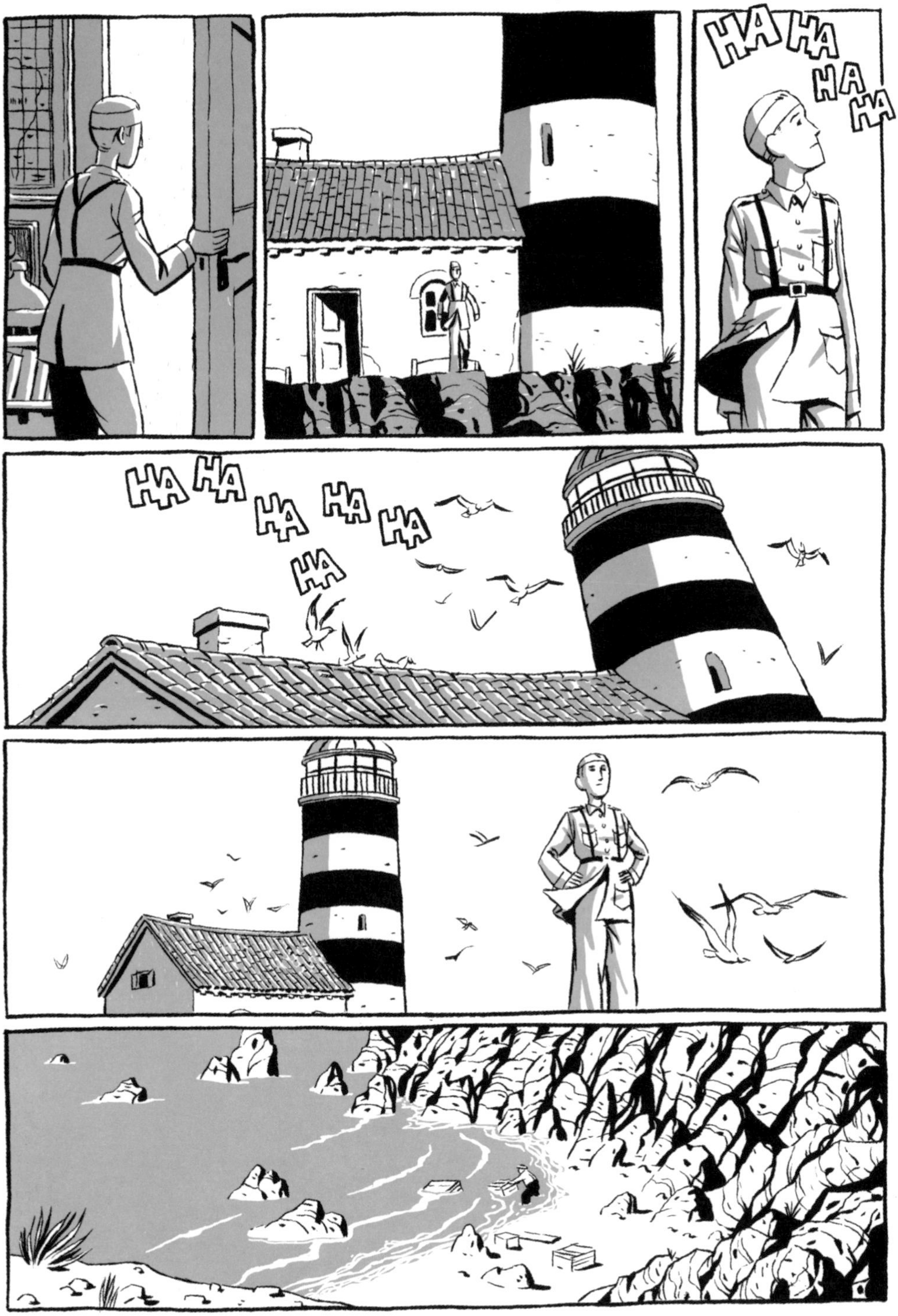
HA HA HA HA
HA HA HA HA HA HA

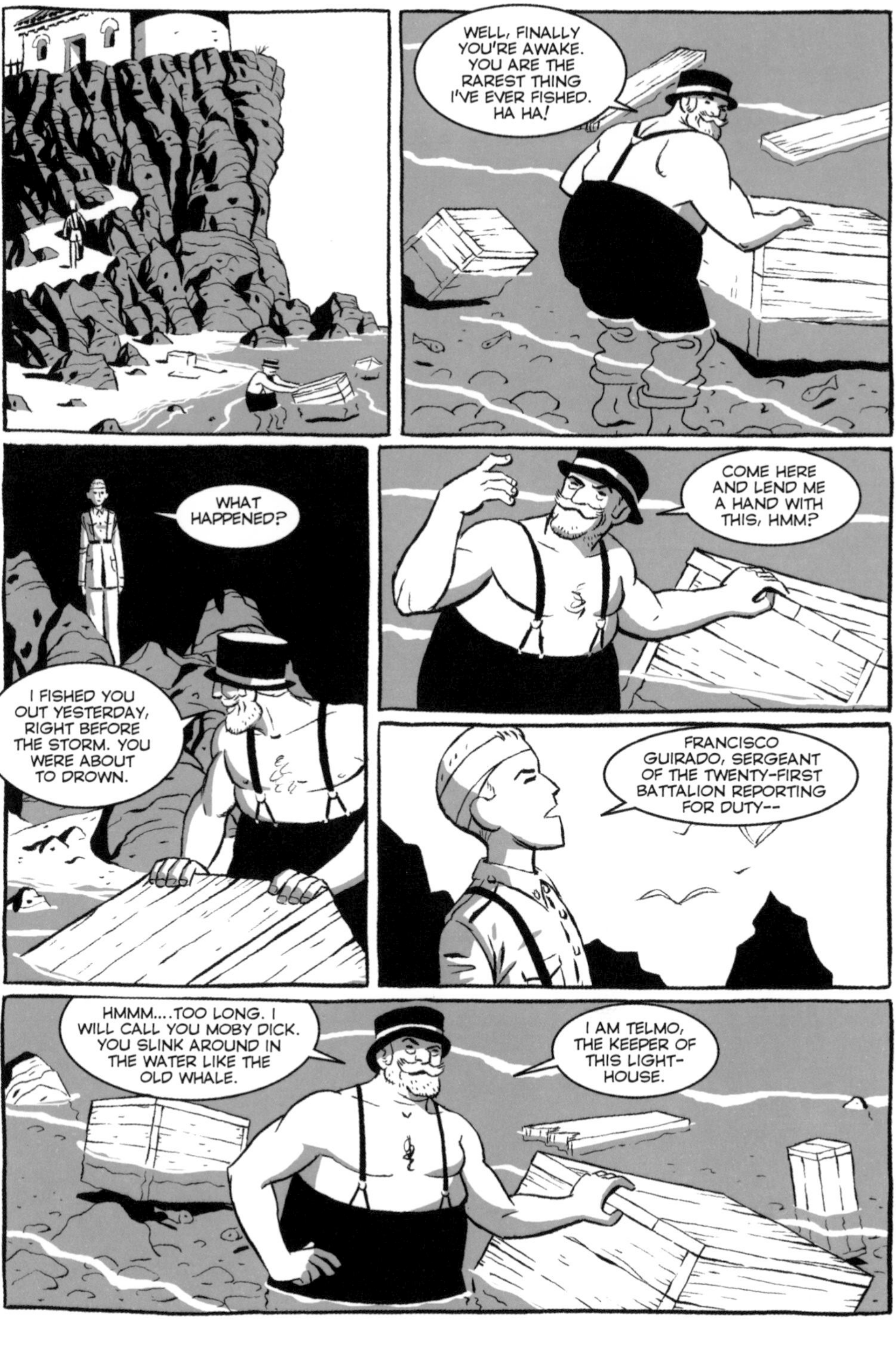
WELL, FINALLY YOU'RE AWAKE. YOU ARE THE RAREST THING I'VE EVER FISHED. HA HA!
WHAT HAPPENED?
I FISHED YOU OUT YESTERDAY, RIGHT BEFORE THE STORM. YOU WERE ABOUT TO DROWN.
COME HERE AND LEND ME A HAND WITH THIS, HMM?
FRANCISCO GUIRADO, SERGEANT OF THE TWENTY-FIRST BATTALION REPORTING FOR DUTY--
HMMM....TOO LONG. I WILL CALL YOU MOBY DICK. YOU SLINK AROUND IN THE WATER LIKE THE OLD WHALE.
I AM TELMO, THE KEEPER OF THIS LIGHT-HOUSE.

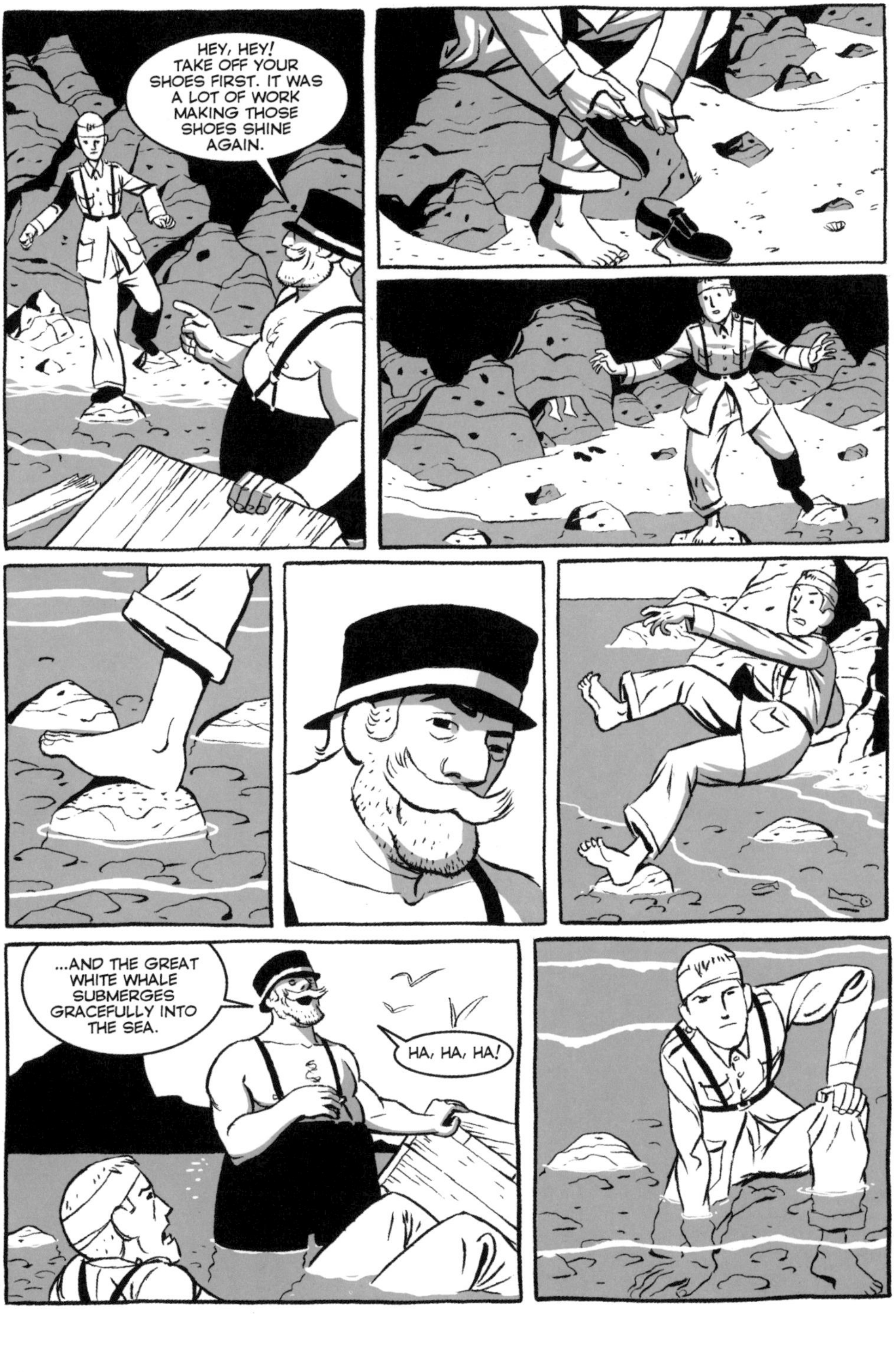
HEY, HEY! TAKE OFF YOUR SHOES FIRST. IT WAS A LOT OF WORK MAKING THOSE SHOES SHINE AGAIN.
...AND THE GREAT WHITE WHALE SUBMERGES GRACEFULLY INTO THE SEA.
HA, HA, HA!

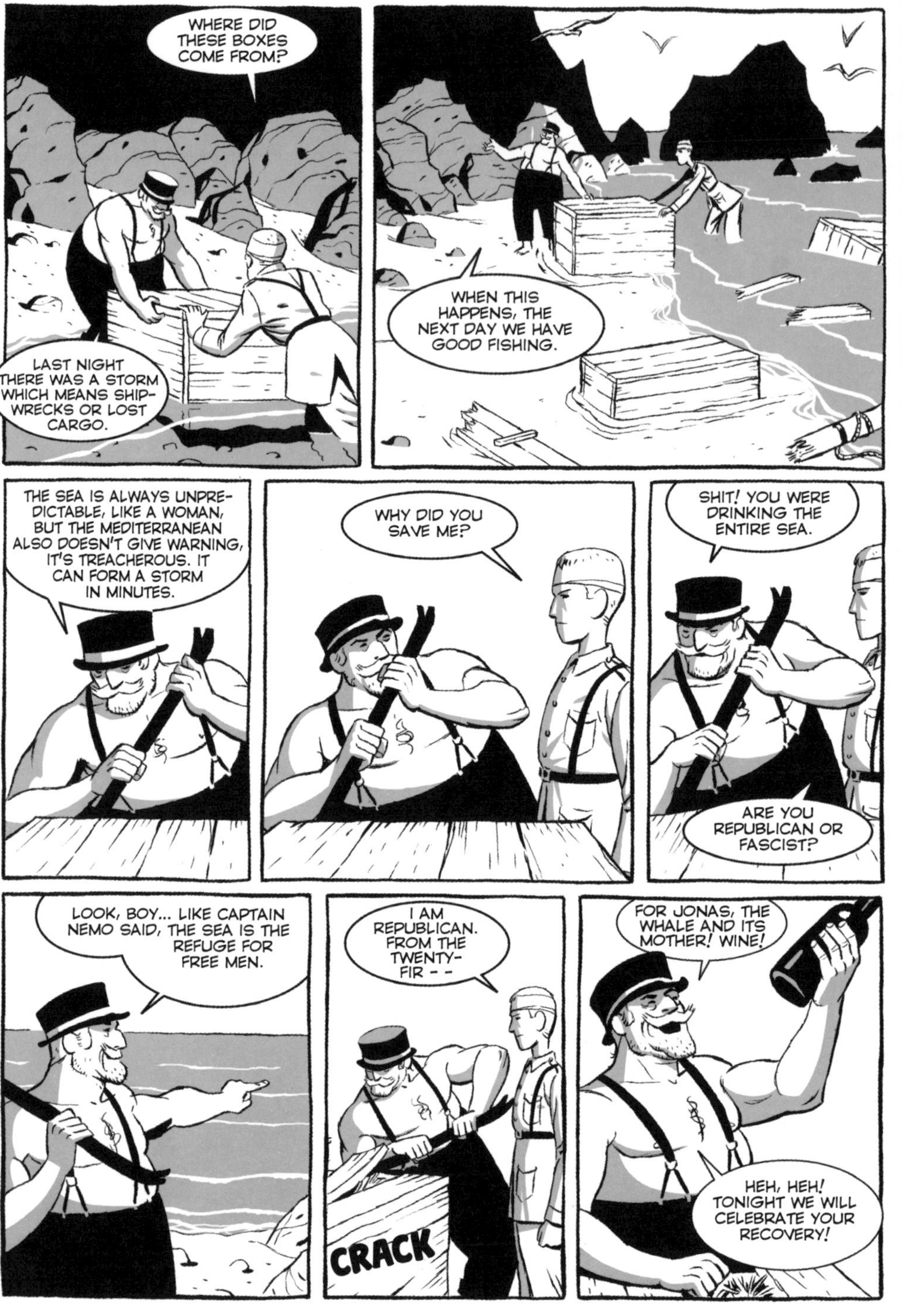
WHERE DID THESE BOXES COME FROM?
LAST NIGHT THERE WAS A STORM WHICH MEANS SHIP-WRECKS OR LOST CARGO.
WHEN THIS HAPPENS, THE NEXT DAY WE HAVE GOOD FISHING.
THE SEA IS ALWAYS UNPRE-DICTABLE, LIKE A WOMAN, BUT THE MEDITERRANEAN ALSO DOESN'T GIVE WARNING, IT'S TREACHEROUS. IT CAN FORM A STORM IN MINUTES.
WHY DID YOU SAVE ME?
SHIT! YOU WERE DRINKING THE ENTIRE SEA.
ARE YOU REPUBLICAN OR FASCIST?
LOOK, BOY... LIKE CAPTAIN NEMO SAID, THE SEA IS THE REFUGE FOR FREE MEN.
I AM REPUBLICAN. FROM THE TWENTY-FIR - -
CRACK
FOR JONAS, THE WHALE AND ITS MOTHER! WINE!
HEH, HEH! TONIGHT WE WILL CELEBRATE YOUR RECOVERY!

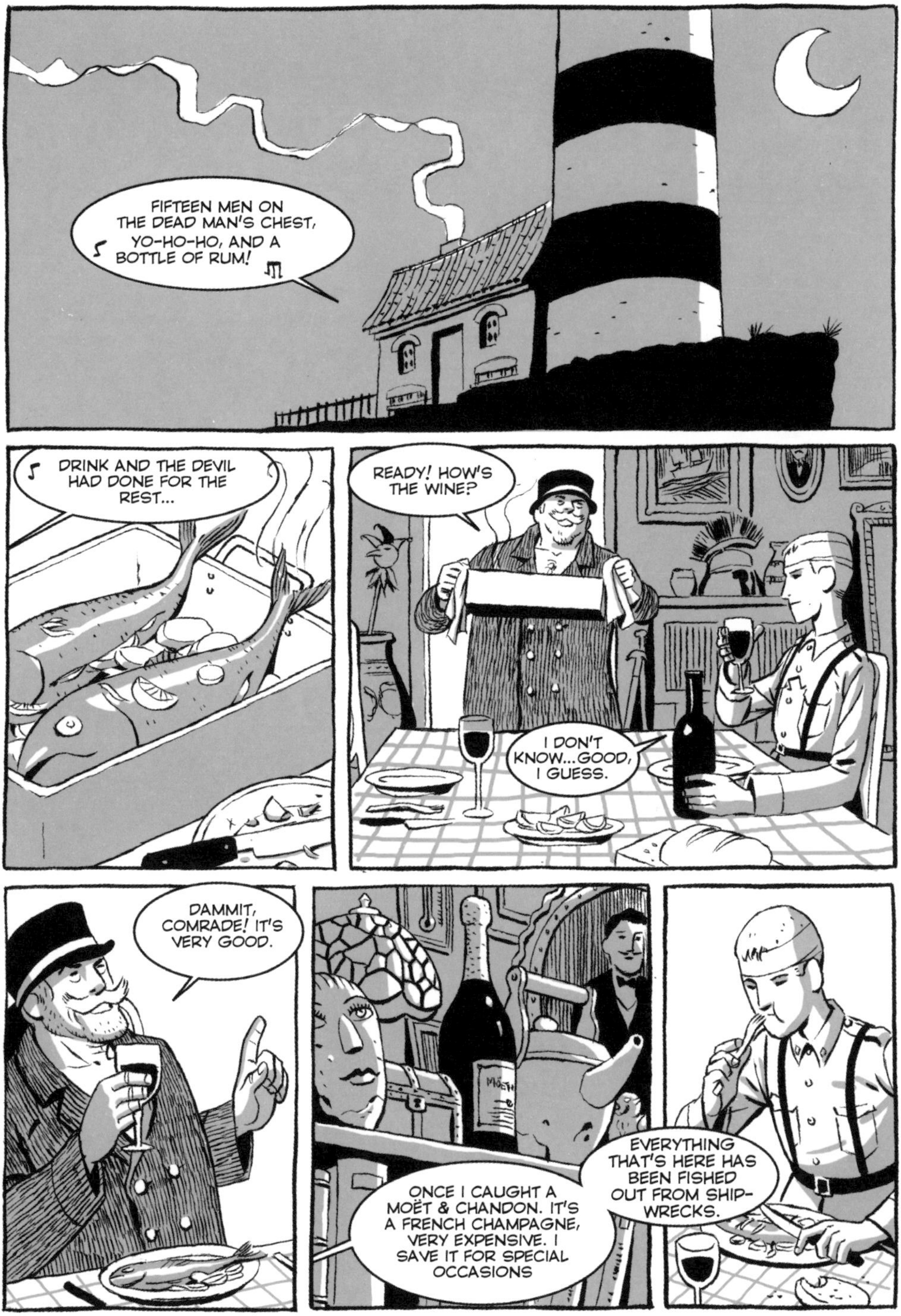
FIFTEEN MEN ON THE DEAD MAN'S CHEST, YO-HO-HO, AND A BOTTLE OF RUM!
DRINK AND THE DEVIL HAD DONE FOR THE REST...
READY! HOW'S THE WINE?
I DON'T KNOW...GOOD, I GUESS.
DAMMIT, COMRADE! IT'S VERY GOOD.
ONCE I CAUGHT A MOËT & CHANDON. IT'S A FRENCH CHAMPAGNE, VERY EXPENSIVE. I SAVE IT FOR SPECIAL OCCASIONS
EVERYTHING THAT'S HERE HAS BEEN FISHED OUT FROM SHIP-WRECKS.

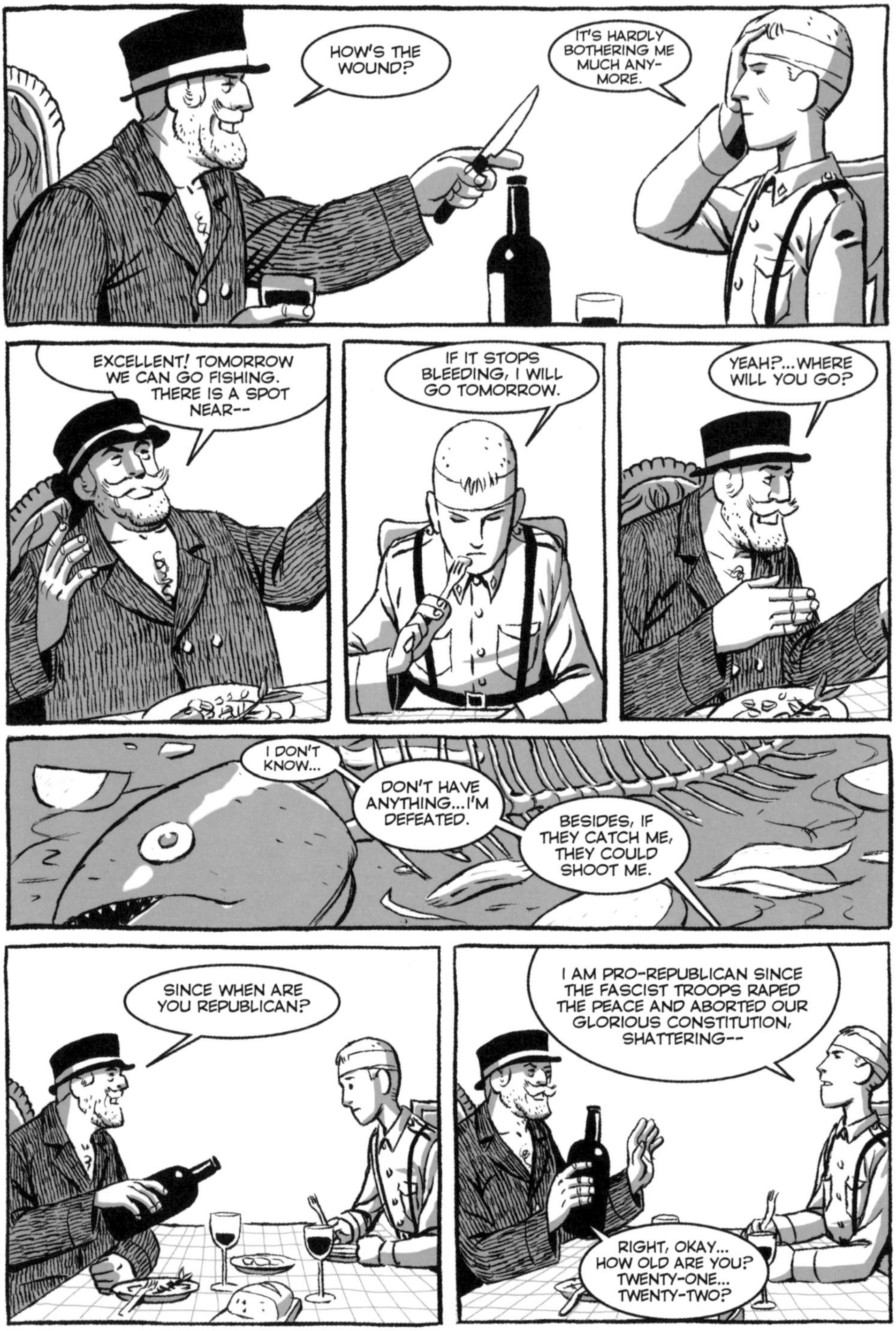
HOW'S THE WOUND?
IT'S HARDLY BOTHERING ME MUCH ANY-MORE.
EXCELLENT! TOMORROW WE CAN GO FISHING. THERE IS A SPOT NEAR--
IF IT STOPS BLEEDING, I WILL GO TOMORROW.
YEAH?...WHERE WILL YOU GO?
I DON'T KNOW...
DON'T HAVE ANYTHING...I'M DEFEATED.
BESIDES, IF THEY CATCH ME, THEY COULD SHOOT ME.
SINCE WHEN ARE YOU REPUBLICAN?
I AM PRO-REPUBLICAN SINCE THE FASCIST TROOPS RAPED THE PEACE AND ABORTED OUR GLORIOUS CONSTITUTION, SHATTERING--
RIGHT, OKAY... HOW OLD ARE YOU? TWENTY-ONE... TWENTY-TWO?

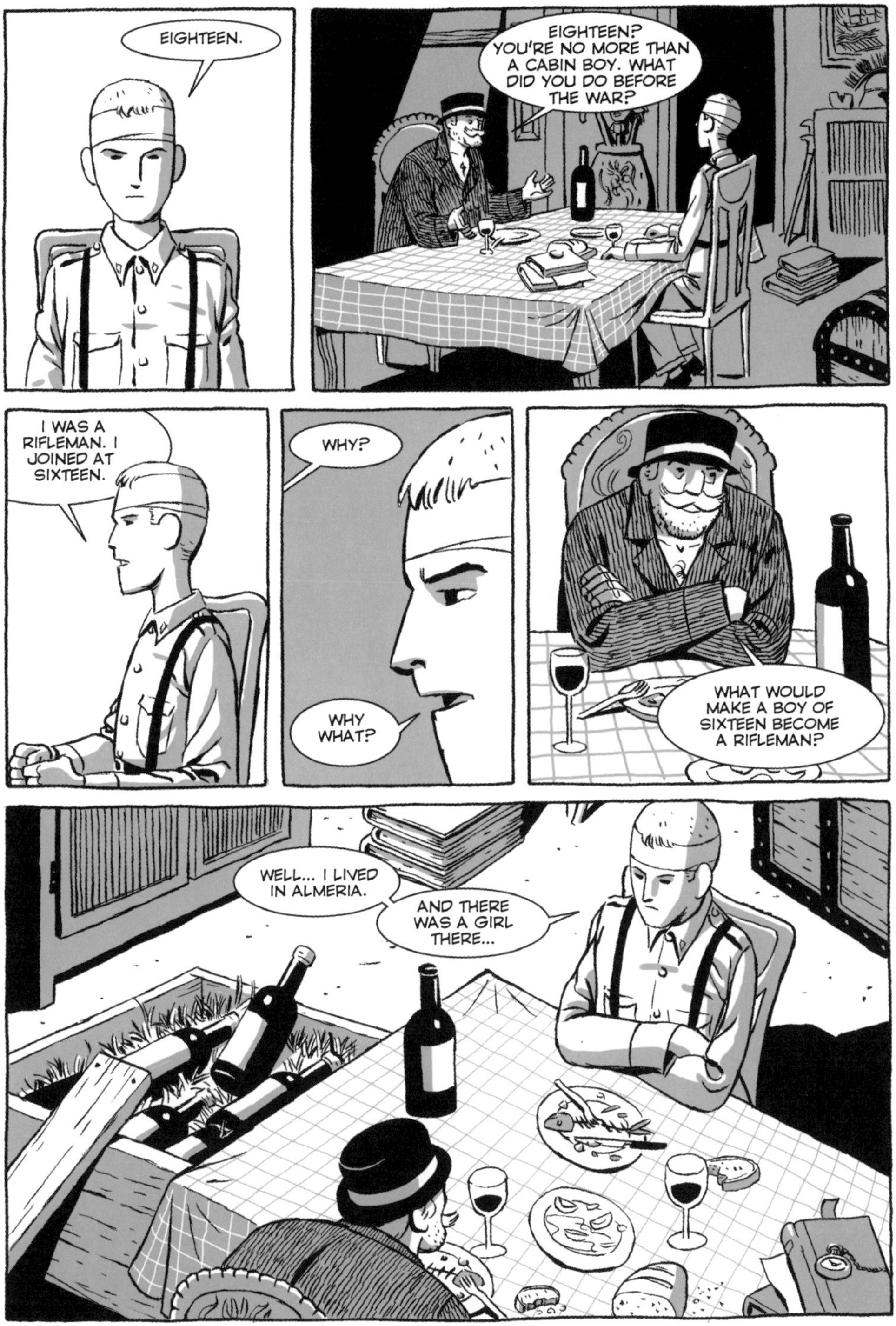
EIGHTEEN.
EIGHTEEN? YOU'RE NO MORE THAN A CABIN BOY. WHAT DID YOU DO BEFORE THE WAR?
I WAS A RIFLEMAN. I JOINED AT SIXTEEN.
WHY?
WHY WHAT?
WHAT WOULD MAKE A BOY OF SIXTEEN BECOME A RIFLEMAN?
WELL... I LIVED IN ALMERIA.
AND THERE WAS A GIRL THERE...

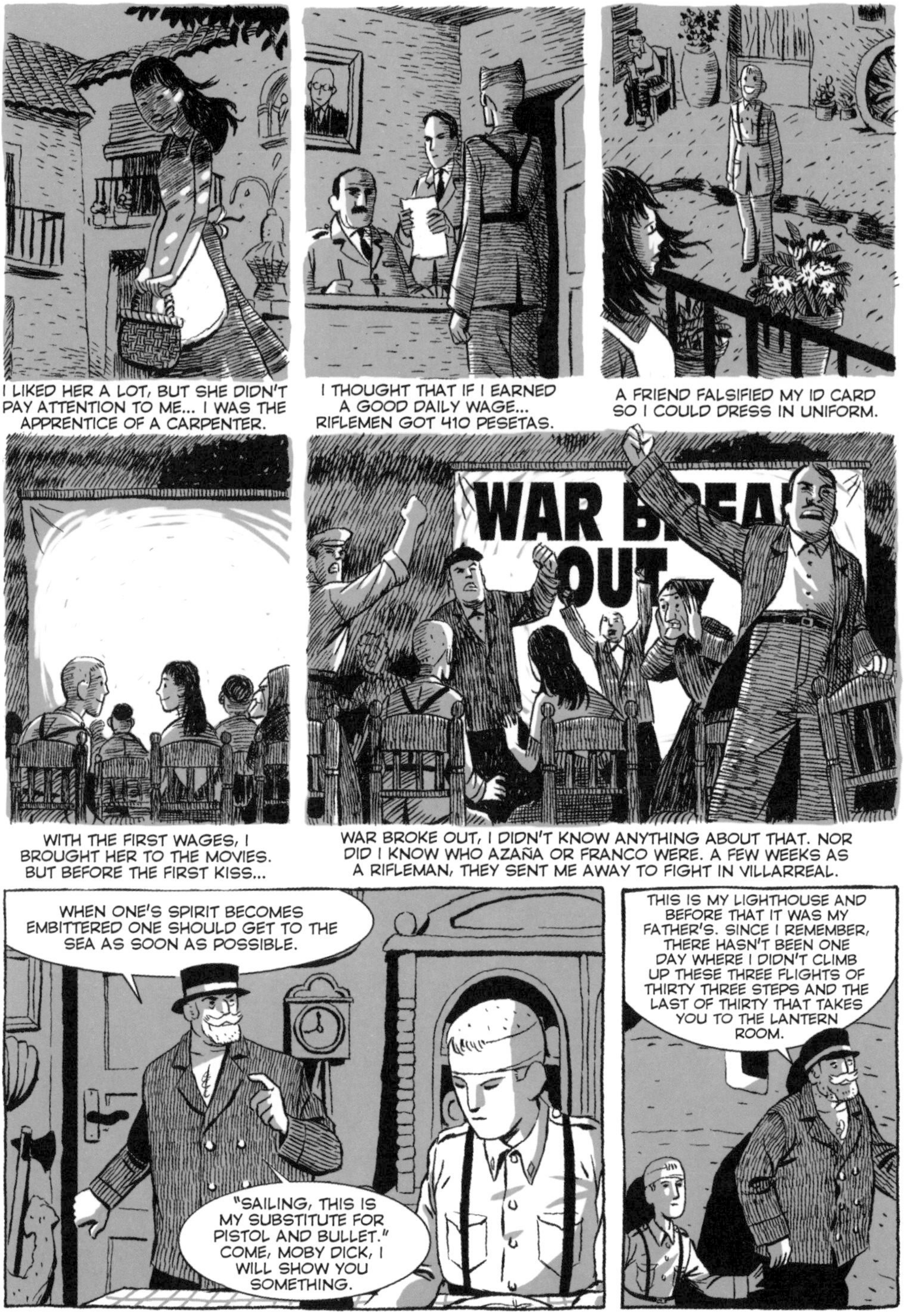
I LIKED HER A LOT, BUT SHE DIDN'T PAY ATTENTION TO ME... I WAS THE APPRENTICE OF A CARPENTER.
I THOUGHT THAT IF I EARNED A GOOD DAILY WAGE... RIFLEMEN GOT 410 PESETAS.
A FRIEND FALSIFIED MY ID CARD SO I COULD DRESS IN UNIFORM.
WITH THE FIRST WAGES, I BROUGHT HER TO THE MOVIES. BUT BEFORE THE FIRST KISS...
WAR BROKE OUT, I DIDN'T KNOW ANYTHING ABOUT THAT. NOR DID I KNOW WHO AZAÑA OR FRANCO WERE. A FEW WEEKS AS A RIFLEMAN, THEY SENT ME AWAY TO FIGHT IN VILLARREAL.
WHEN ONE'S SPIRIT BECOMES EMBITTERED ONE SHOULD GET TO THE SEA AS SOON AS POSSIBLE.
"SAILING, THIS IS MY SUBSTITUTE FOR PISTOL AND BULLET." COME, MOBY DICK, I WILL SHOW YOU SOMETHING.
THIS IS MY LIGHTHOUSE AND BEFORE THAT IT WAS MY FATHER'S. SINCE I REMEMBER, THERE HASN'T BEEN ONE DAY WHERE I DIDN'T CLIMB UP THESE THREE FLIGHTS OF THIRTY THREE STEPS AND THE LAST OF THIRTY THAT TAKES YOU TO THE LANTERN ROOM.

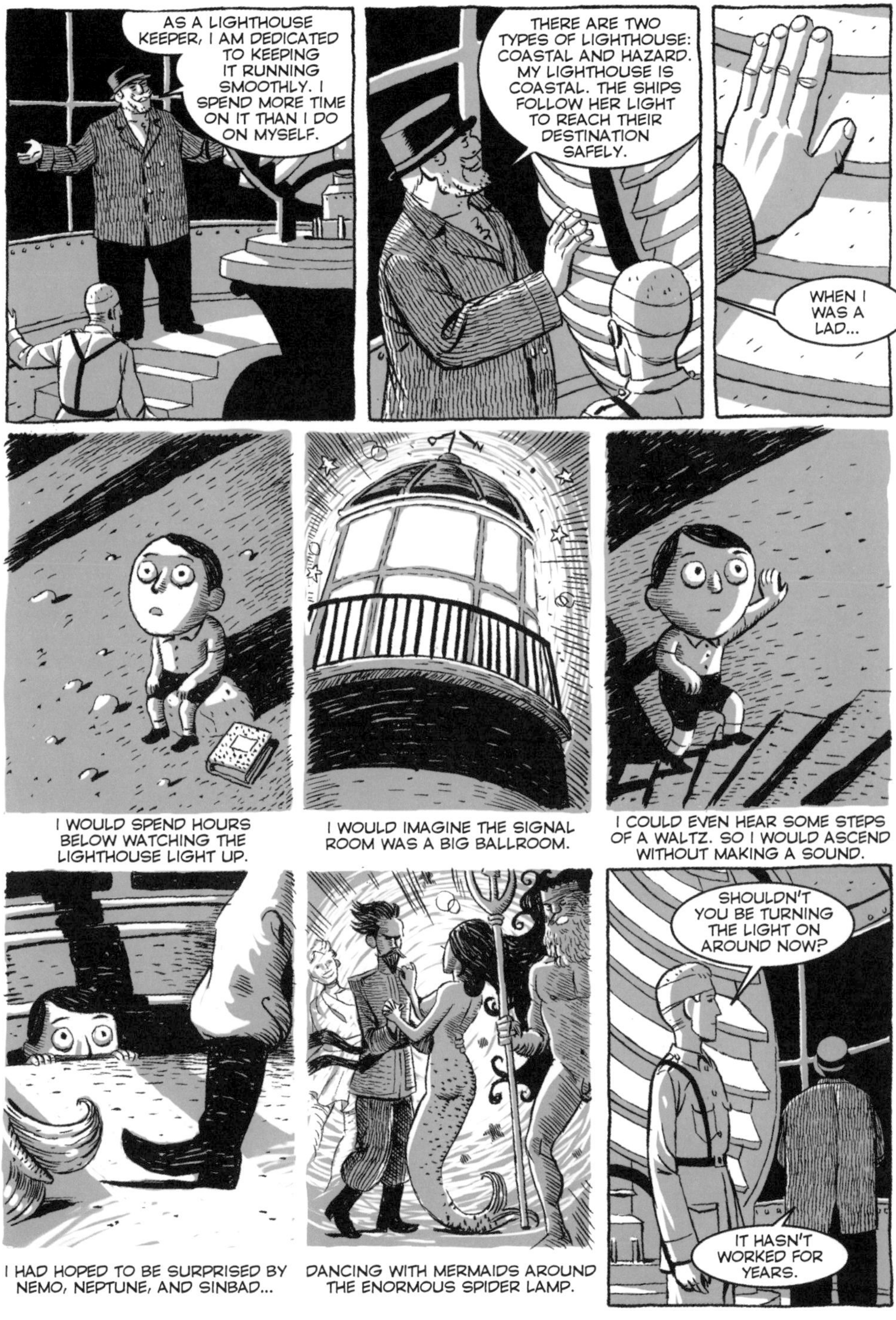
AS A LIGHTHOUSE KEEPER, I AM DEDICATED TO KEEPING IT RUNNING SMOOTHLY. I SPEND MORE TIME ON IT THAN I DO ON MYSELF.
THERE ARE TWO TYPES OF LIGHTHOUSE: COASTAL AND HAZARD. MY LIGHTHOUSE IS COASTAL. THE SHIPS FOLLOW HER LIGHT TO REACH THEIR DESTINATION SAFELY.
WHEN I WAS A LAD...
I WOULD SPEND HOURS BELOW WATCHING THE LIGHTHOUSE LIGHT UP.
I WOULD IMAGINE THE SIGNAL ROOM WAS A BIG BALLROOM.
I COULD EVEN HEAR SOME STEPS OF A WALTZ. SO I WOULD ASCEND WITHOUT MAKING A SOUND.
I HAD HOPED TO BE SURPRISED BY NEMO, NEPTUNE, AND SINBAD...
DANCING WITH MERMAIDS AROUND THE ENORMOUS SPIDER LAMP.
SHOULDN'T YOU BE TURNING THE LIGHT ON AROUND NOW?
IT HASN'T WORKED FOR YEARS.

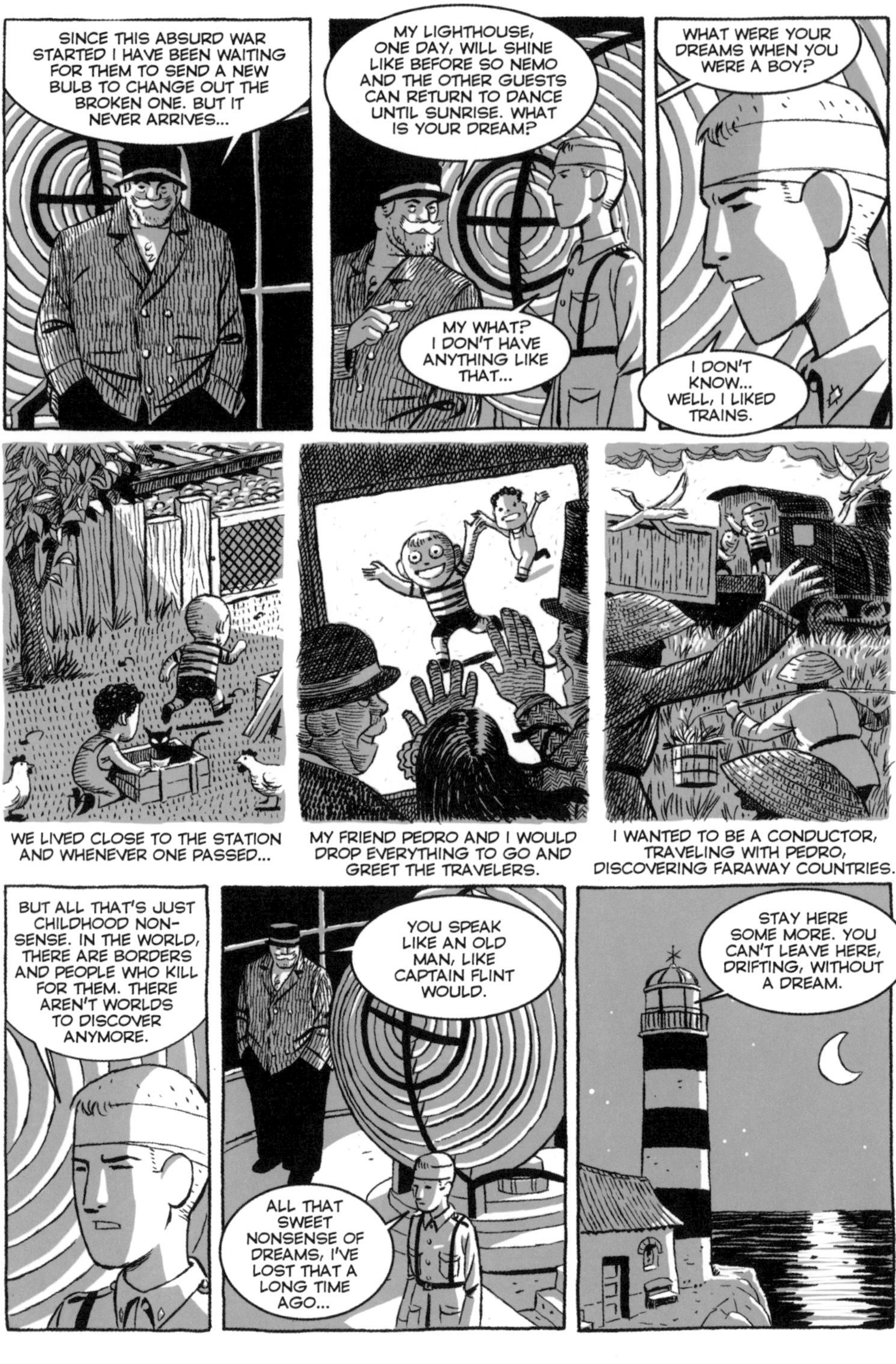
SINCE THIS ABSURD WAR STARTED I HAVE BEEN WAITING FOR THEM TO SEND A NEW BULB TO CHANGE OUT THE BROKEN ONE. BUT IT NEVER ARRIVES...
MY LIGHTHOUSE, ONE DAY, WILL SHINE LIKE BEFORE SO NEMO AND THE OTHER GUESTS CAN RETURN TO DANCE UNTIL SUNRISE. WHAT IS YOUR DREAM?
MY WHAT? I DON'T HAVE ANYTHING LIKE THAT...
WHAT WERE YOUR DREAMS WHEN YOU WERE A BOY?
I DON'T KNOW... WELL, I LIKED TRAINS.
WE LIVED CLOSE TO THE STATION AND WHENEVER ONE PASSED...
MY FRIEND PEDRO AND I WOULD DROP EVERYTHING TO GO AND GREET THE TRAVELERS.
I WANTED TO BE A CONDUCTOR, TRAVELING WITH PEDRO, DISCOVERING FARAWAY COUNTRIES.
BUT ALL THAT'S JUST CHILDHOOD NON-SENSE. IN THE WORLD, THERE ARE BORDERS AND PEOPLE WHO KILL FOR THEM. THERE AREN'T WORLDS TO DISCOVER ANYMORE.
YOU SPEAK LIKE AN OLD MAN, LIKE CAPTAIN FLINT WOULD.
ALL THAT SWEET NONSENSE OF DREAMS, I'VE LOST THAT A LONG TIME AGO...
STAY HERE SOME MORE. YOU CAN'T LEAVE HERE, DRIFTING, WITHOUT A DREAM.

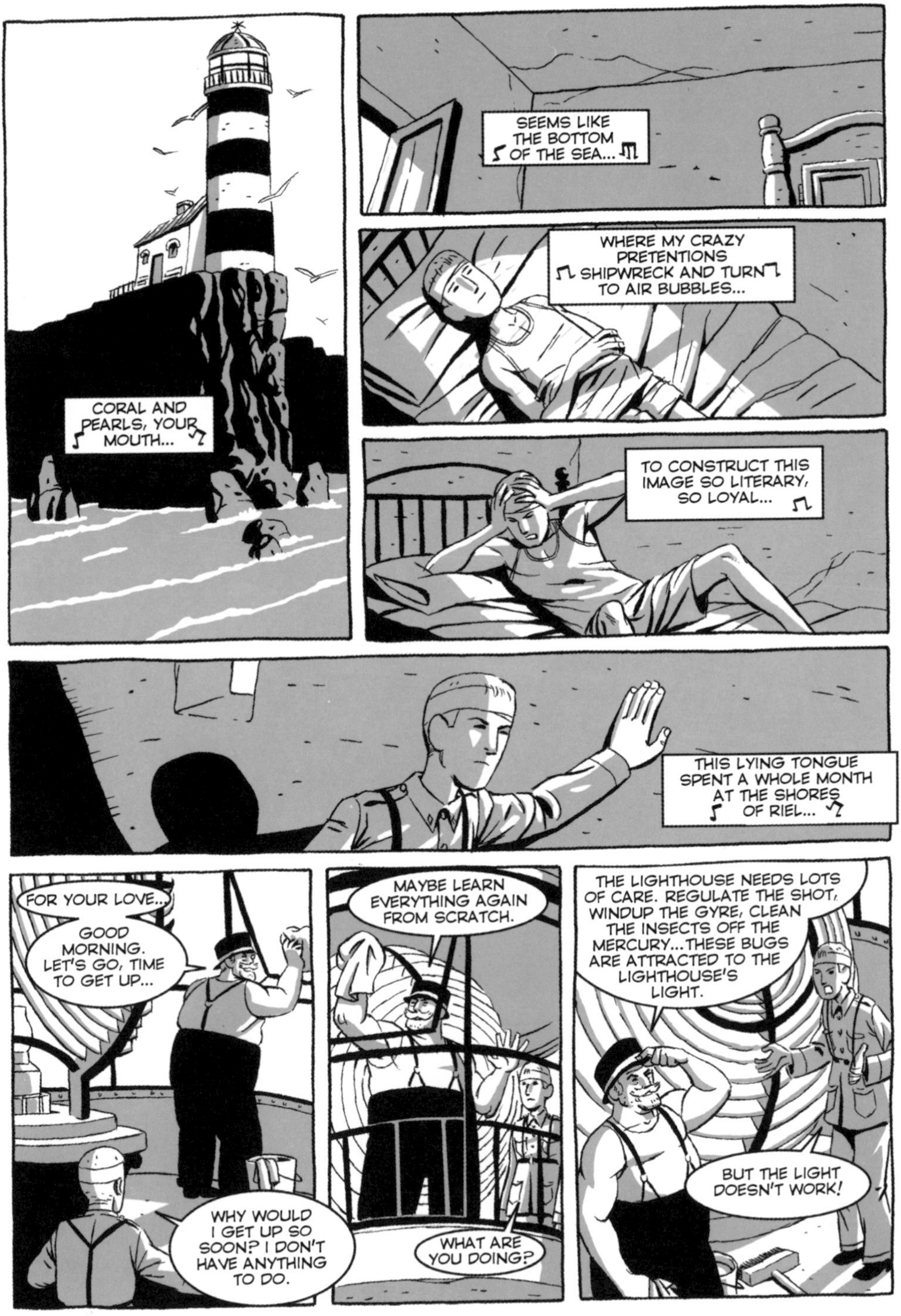
CORAL AND PEARLS, YOUR MOUTH...
SEEMS LIKE THE BOTTOM OF THE SEA...
WHERE MY CRAZY PRETENTIONS SHIPWRECK AND TURN TO AIR BUBBLES...
TO CONSTRUCT THIS IMAGE SO LITERARY, SO LOYAL...
THIS LYING TONGUE SPENT A WHOLE MONTH AT THE SHORES OF RIEL...
FOR YOUR LOVE...
GOOD MORNING. LET'S GO, TIME TO GET UP...
WHY WOULD I GET UP SO SOON? I DON'T HAVE ANYTHING TO DO.
MAYBE LEARN EVERYTHING AGAIN FROM SCRATCH.
WHAT ARE YOU DOING?
THE LIGHTHOUSE NEEDS LOTS OF CARE. REGULATE THE SHOT, WINDUP THE GYRE, CLEAN THE INSECTS OFF THE MERCURY...THESE BUGS ARE ATTRACTED TO THE LIGHTHOUSE'S LIGHT.
BUT THE LIGHT DOESN'T WORK!

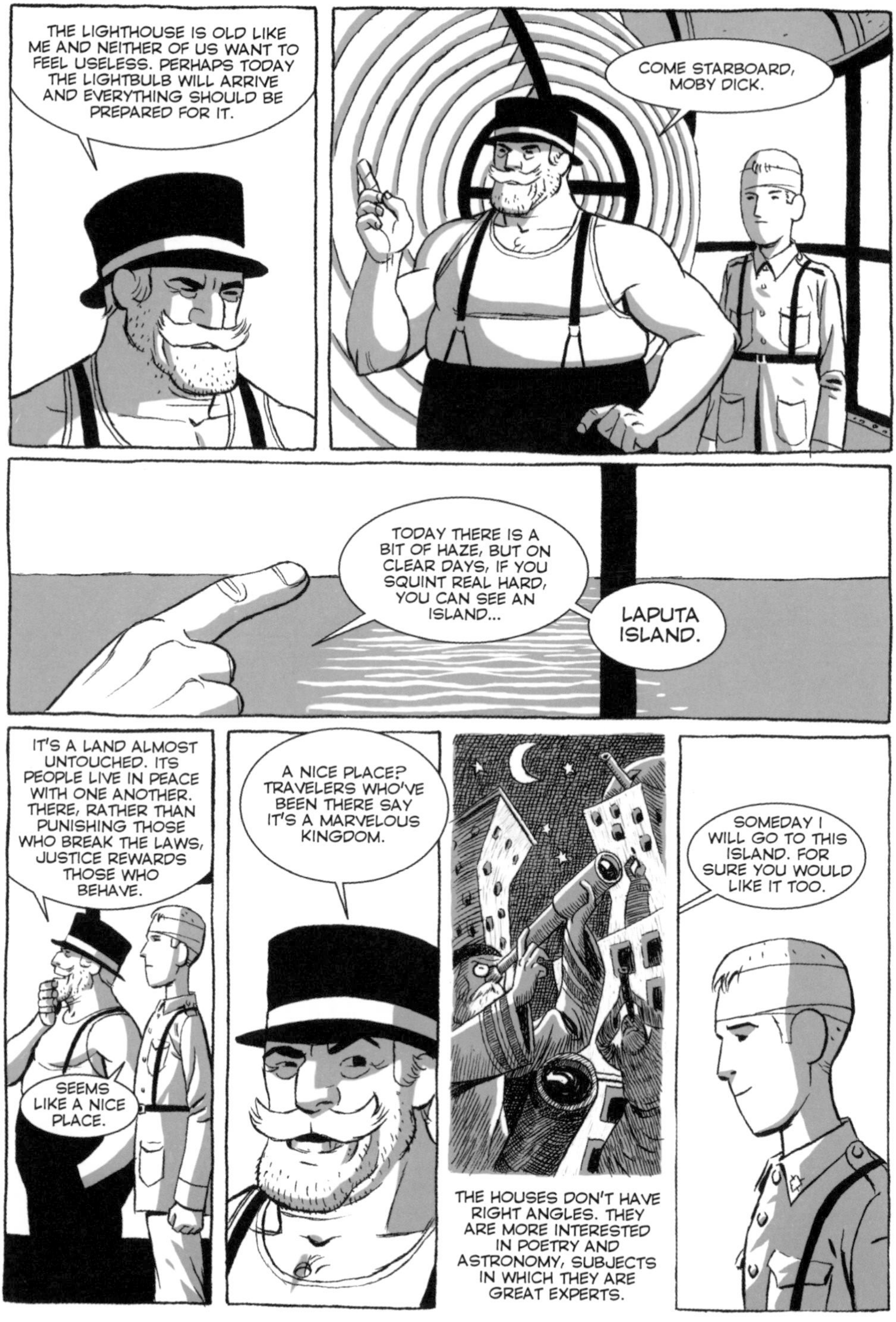

THE LIGHTHOUSE IS OLD LIKE ME AND NEITHER OF US WANT TO FEEL USELESS. PERHAPS TODAY THE LIGHTBULB WILL ARRIVE AND EVERYTHING SHOULD BE PREPARED FOR IT.
COME STARBOARD, MOBY DICK.
TODAY THERE IS A BIT OF HAZE, BUT ON CLEAR DAYS, IF YOU SQUINT REAL HARD, YOU CAN SEE AN ISLAND...
LAPUTA ISLAND.
IT'S A LAND ALMOST UNTOUCHED. ITS PEOPLE LIVE IN PEACE WITH ONE ANOTHER. THERE, RATHER THAN PUNISHING THOSE WHO BREAK THE LAWS, JUSTICE REWARDS THOSE WHO BEHAVE.
SEEMS LIKE A NICE PLACE.
A NICE PLACE? TRAVELERS WHO'VE BEEN THERE SAY IT'S A MARVELOUS KINGDOM.
THE HOUSES DON'T HAVE RIGHT ANGLES. THEY ARE MORE INTERESTED IN POETRY AND ASTRONOMY, SUBJECTS IN WHICH THEY ARE GREAT EXPERTS.
SOMEDAY I WILL GO TO THIS ISLAND. FOR SURE YOU WOULD LIKE IT TOO.

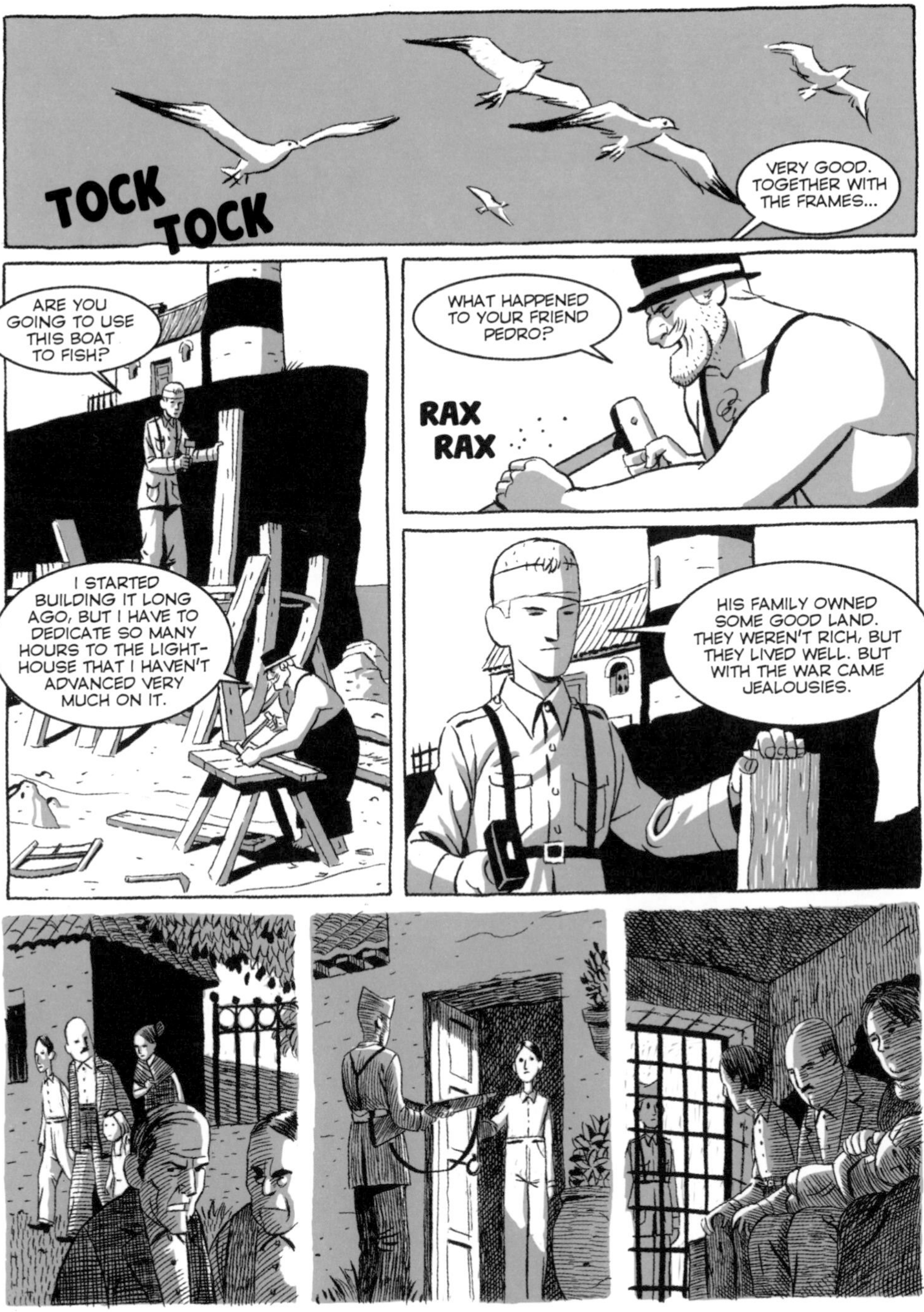
TOCK
TOCK
VERY GOOD. TOGETHER WITH THE FRAMES...
ARE YOU GOING TO USE THIS BOAT TO FISH?
I STARTED BUILDING IT LONG AGO, BUT I HAVE TO DEDICATE SO MANY HOURS TO THE LIGHT-HOUSE THAT I HAVEN'T ADVANCED VERY MUCH ON IT.
WHAT HAPPENED TO YOUR FRIEND PEDRO?
RAX
RAX
HIS FAMILY OWNED SOME GOOD LAND. THEY WEREN'T RICH, BUT THEY LIVED WELL. BUT WITH THE WAR CAME JEALOUSIES.

ANY PERSON WHO HAD MONEY WAS TAKEN FOR A FASCISTA.

ONE OF MY FIRST DUTIES AS RIFLEMAN WAS TO DETAIN PEDRO AND HIS FAMILY.

I DIDN'T KNOW WHAT THEY WOULD DO WITH THEM. JUST A FEW WEEKS BEFORE THEY WERE LIKE ANY OTHER FAMILY.

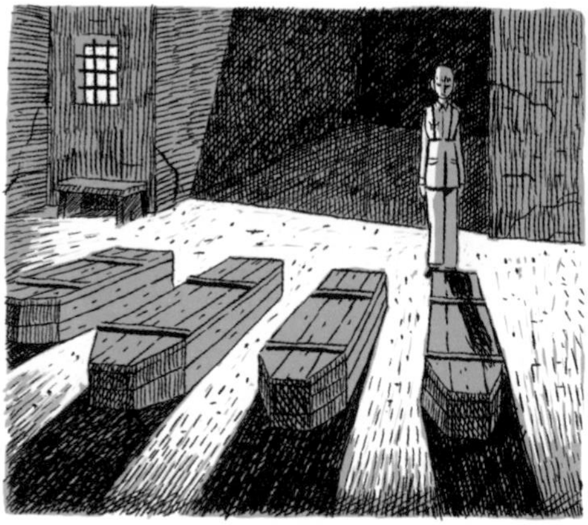

THEY SHOT THEM ALL.

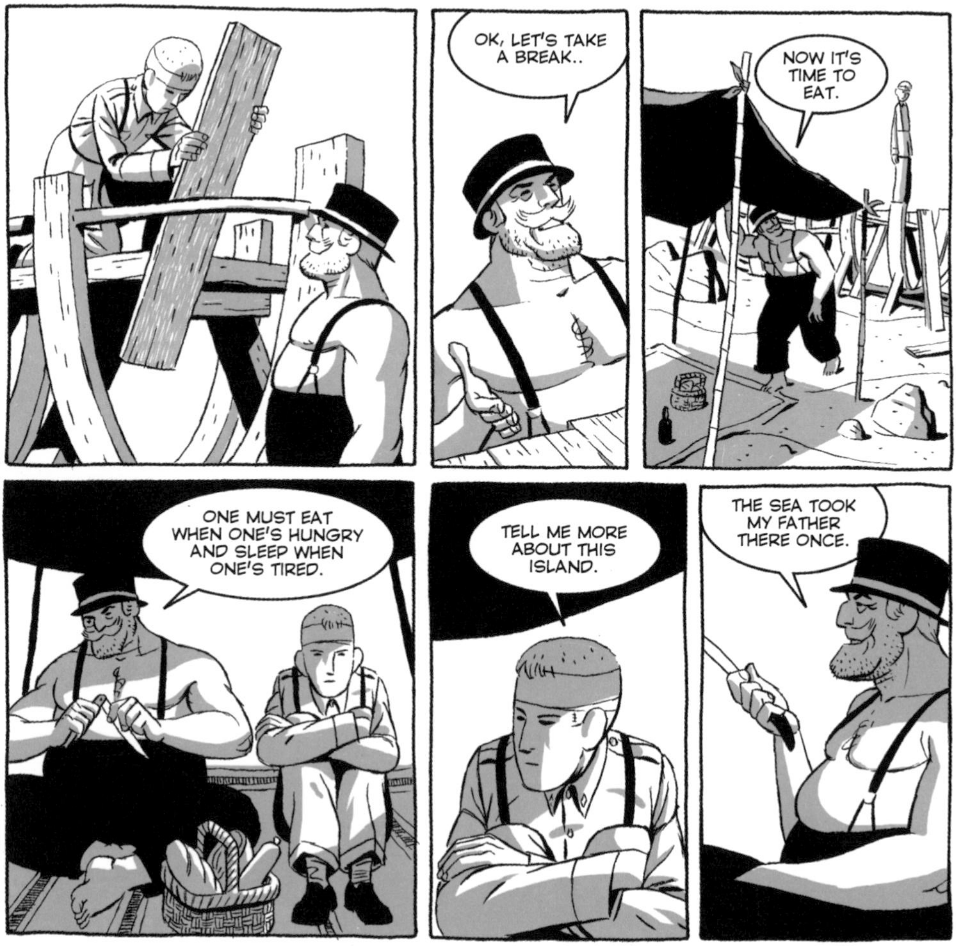

OK, LET'S TAKE A BREAK..
NOW IT'S TIME TO EAT.
ONE MUST EAT WHEN ONE'S HUNGRY AND SLEEP WHEN ONE'S TIRED.
TELL ME MORE ABOUT THIS ISLAND.
THE SEA TOOK MY FATHER THERE ONCE.

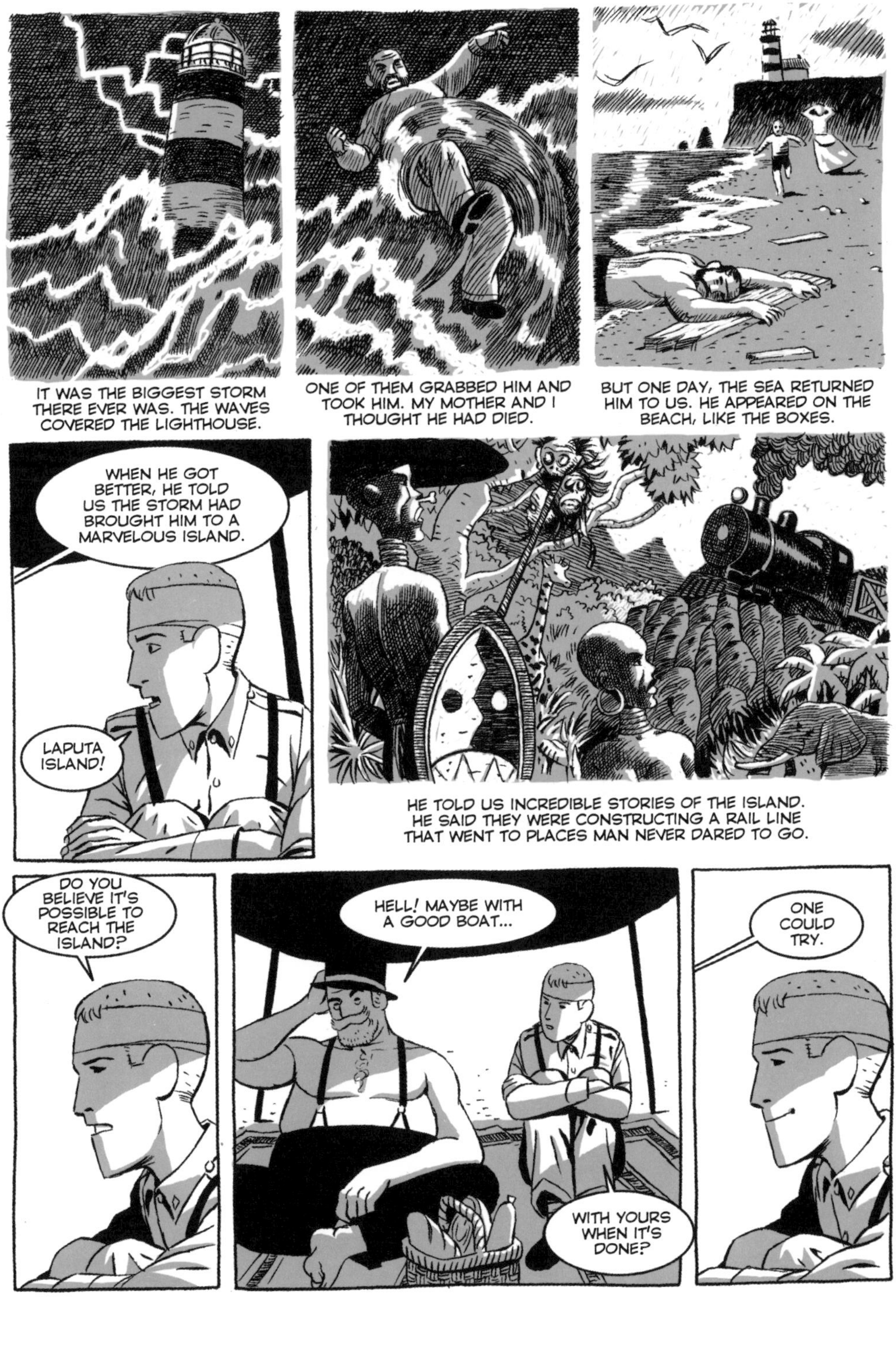
IT WAS THE BIGGEST STORM THERE EVER WAS. THE WAVES COVERED THE LIGHTHOUSE.
ONE OF THEM GRABBED HIM AND TOOK HIM. MY MOTHER AND I THOUGHT HE HAD DIED.
BUT ONE DAY, THE SEA RETURNED HIM TO US. HE APPEARED ON THE BEACH, LIKE THE BOXES.
WHEN HE GOT BETTER, HE TOLD US THE STORM HAD BROUGHT HIM TO A MARVELOUS ISLAND.
LAPUTA ISLAND!
HE TOLD US INCREDIBLE STORIES OF THE ISLAND. HE SAID THEY WERE CONSTRUCTING A RAIL LINE THAT WENT TO PLACES MAN NEVER DARED TO GO.
DO YOU BELIEVE IT'S POSSIBLE TO REACH THE ISLAND?
HELL! MAYBE WITH A GOOD BOAT...
WITH YOURS WHEN IT'S DONE?
ONE COULD TRY.

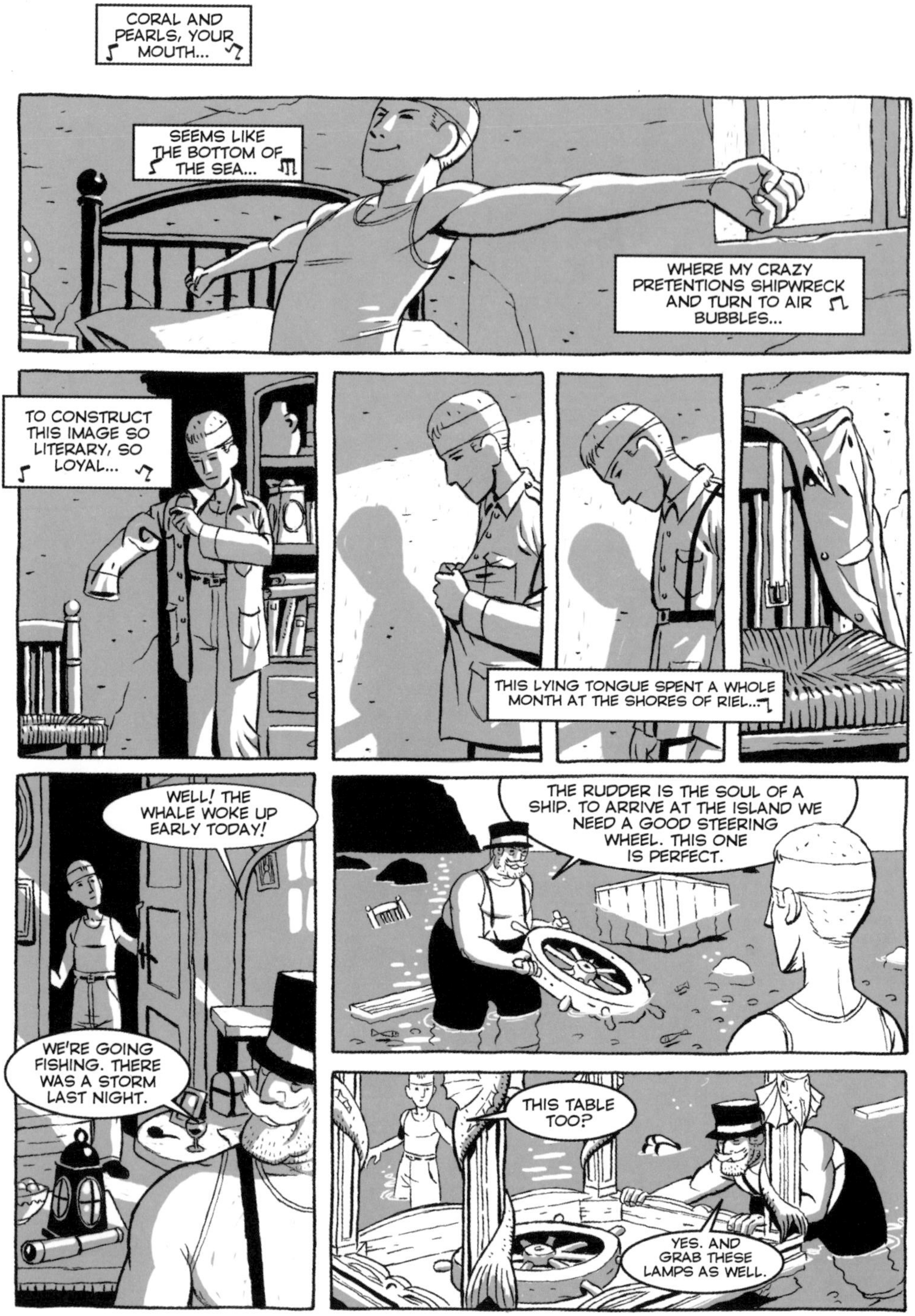
CORAL AND PEARLS, YOUR MOUTH...
SEEMS LIKE THE BOTTOM OF THE SEA...
WHERE MY CRAZY PRETENTIONS SHIPWRECK AND TURN TO AIR BUBBLES...
TO CONSTRUCT THIS IMAGE SO LITERARY, SO LOYAL...
THIS LYING TONGUE SPENT A WHOLE MONTH AT THE SHORES OF RIEL...
WELL! THE WHALE WOKE UP EARLY TODAY!
WE'RE GOING FISHING. THERE WAS A STORM LAST NIGHT.
THE RUDDER IS THE SOUL OF A SHIP. TO ARRIVE AT THE ISLAND WE NEED A GOOD STEERING WHEEL. THIS ONE IS PERFECT.
THIS TABLE TOO?
YES. AND GRAB THESE LAMPS AS WELL.

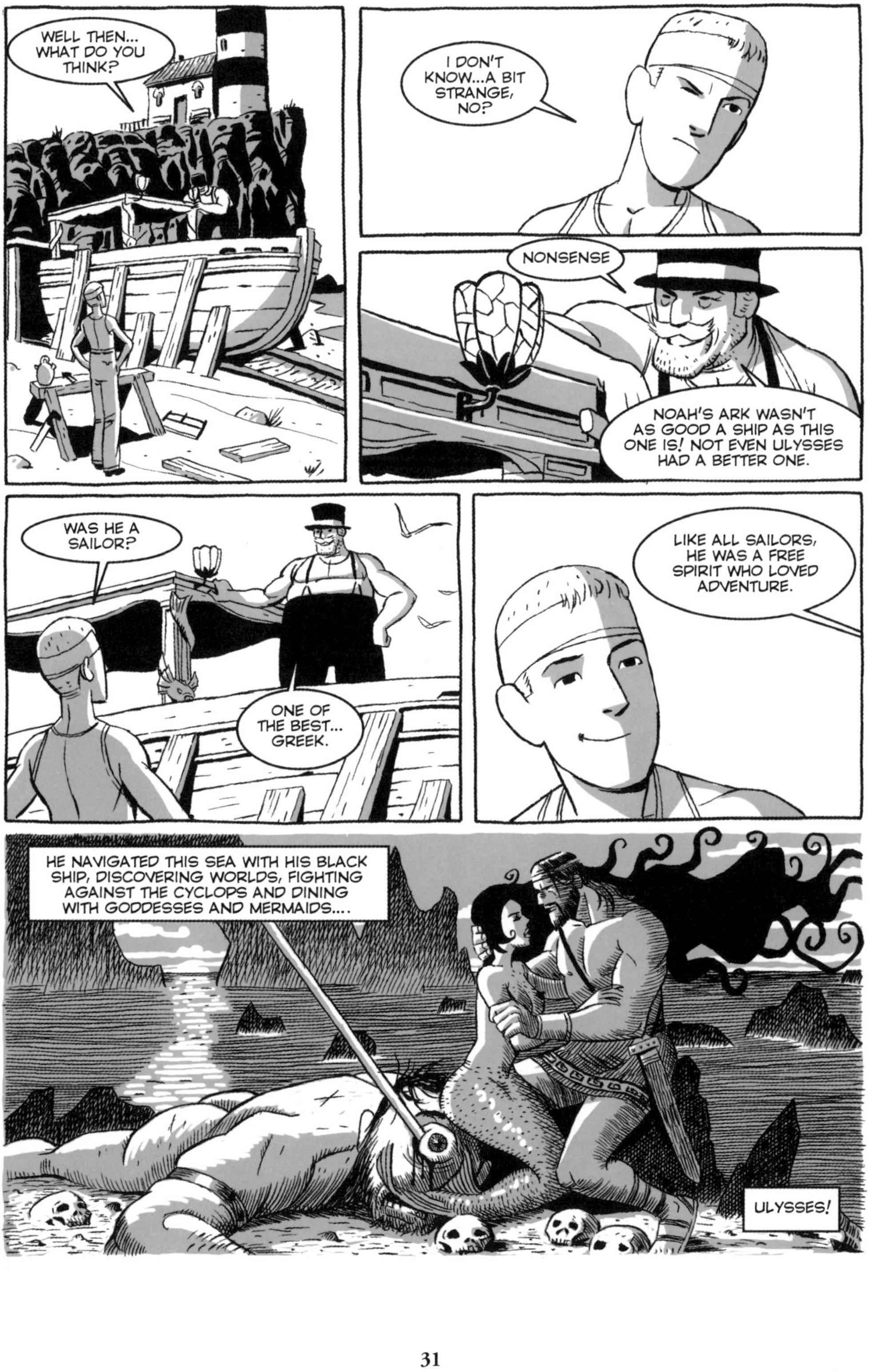
WELL THEN... WHAT DO YOU THINK?
I DON'T KNOW...A BIT STRANGE, NO?
NONSENSE
NOAH'S ARK WASN'T AS GOOD A SHIP AS THIS ONE IS! NOT EVEN ULYSSES HAD A BETTER ONE.
WAS HE A SAILOR?
ONE OF THE BEST... GREEK.
LIKE ALL SAILORS, HE WAS A FREE SPIRIT WHO LOVED ADVENTURE.
HE NAVIGATED THIS SEA WITH HIS BLACK SHIP, DISCOVERING WORLDS, FIGHTING AGAINST THE CYCLOPS AND DINING WITH GODDESSES AND MERMAIDS....
ULYSSES!

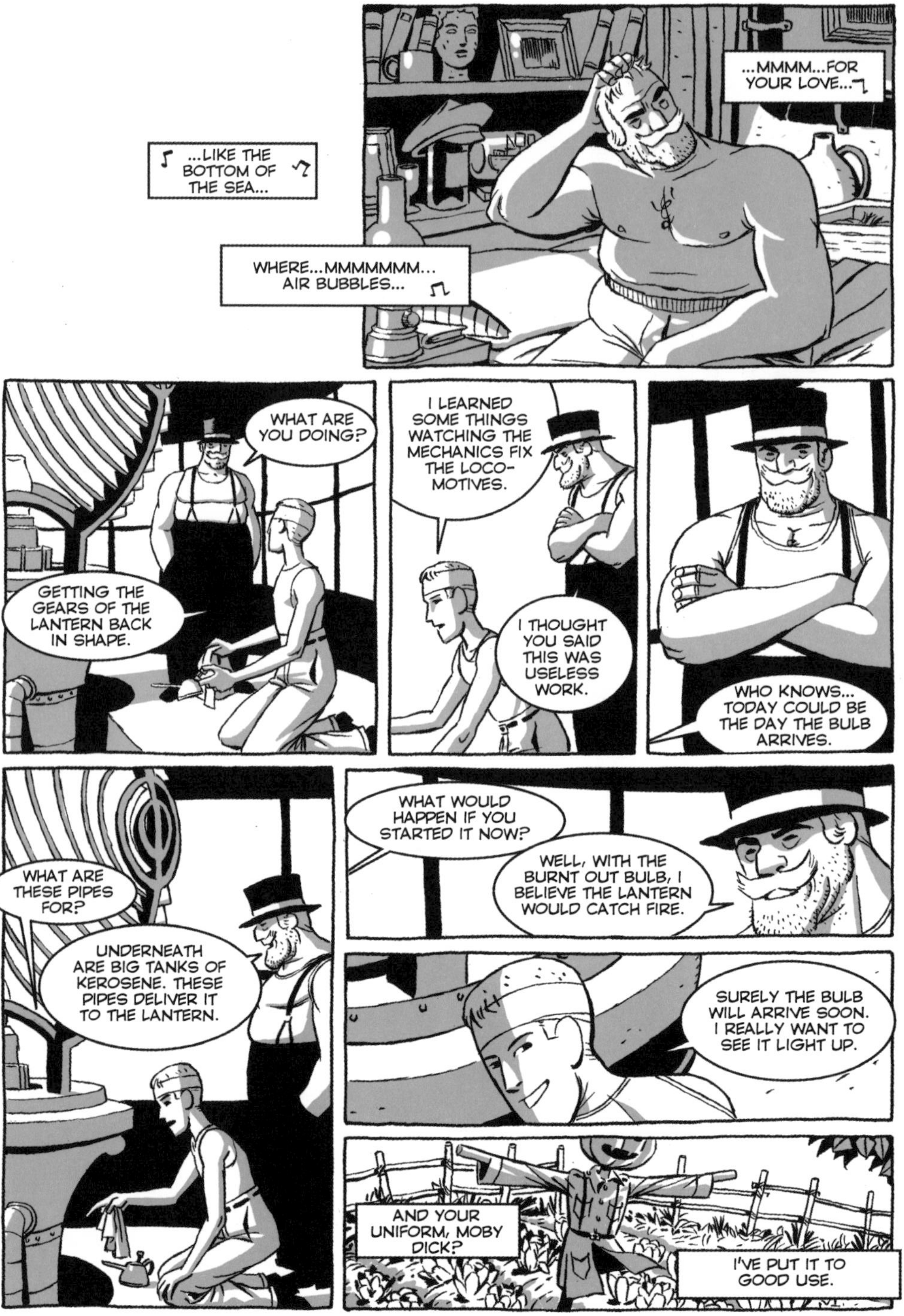
...LIKE THE BOTTOM OF THE SEA...
WHERE...MMMMMMM... AIR BUBBLES...
...MMMM...FOR YOUR LOVE...
WHAT ARE YOU DOING?
GETTING THE GEARS OF THE LANTERN BACK IN SHAPE.
I LEARNED SOME THINGS WATCHING THE MECHANICS FIX THE LOCO-MOTIVES.
I THOUGHT YOU SAID THIS WAS USELESS WORK.
WHO KNOWS... TODAY COULD BE THE DAY THE BULB ARRIVES.
WHAT ARE THESE PIPES FOR?
UNDERNEATH ARE BIG TANKS OF KEROSENE. THESE PIPES DELIVER IT TO THE LANTERN.
WHAT WOULD HAPPEN IF YOU STARTED IT NOW?
WELL, WITH THE BURNT OUT BULB, I BELIEVE THE LANTERN WOULD CATCH FIRE.
SURELY THE BULB WILL ARRIVE SOON. I REALLY WANT TO SEE IT LIGHT UP.
AND YOUR UNIFORM, MOBY DICK?
I'VE PUT IT TO GOOD USE.

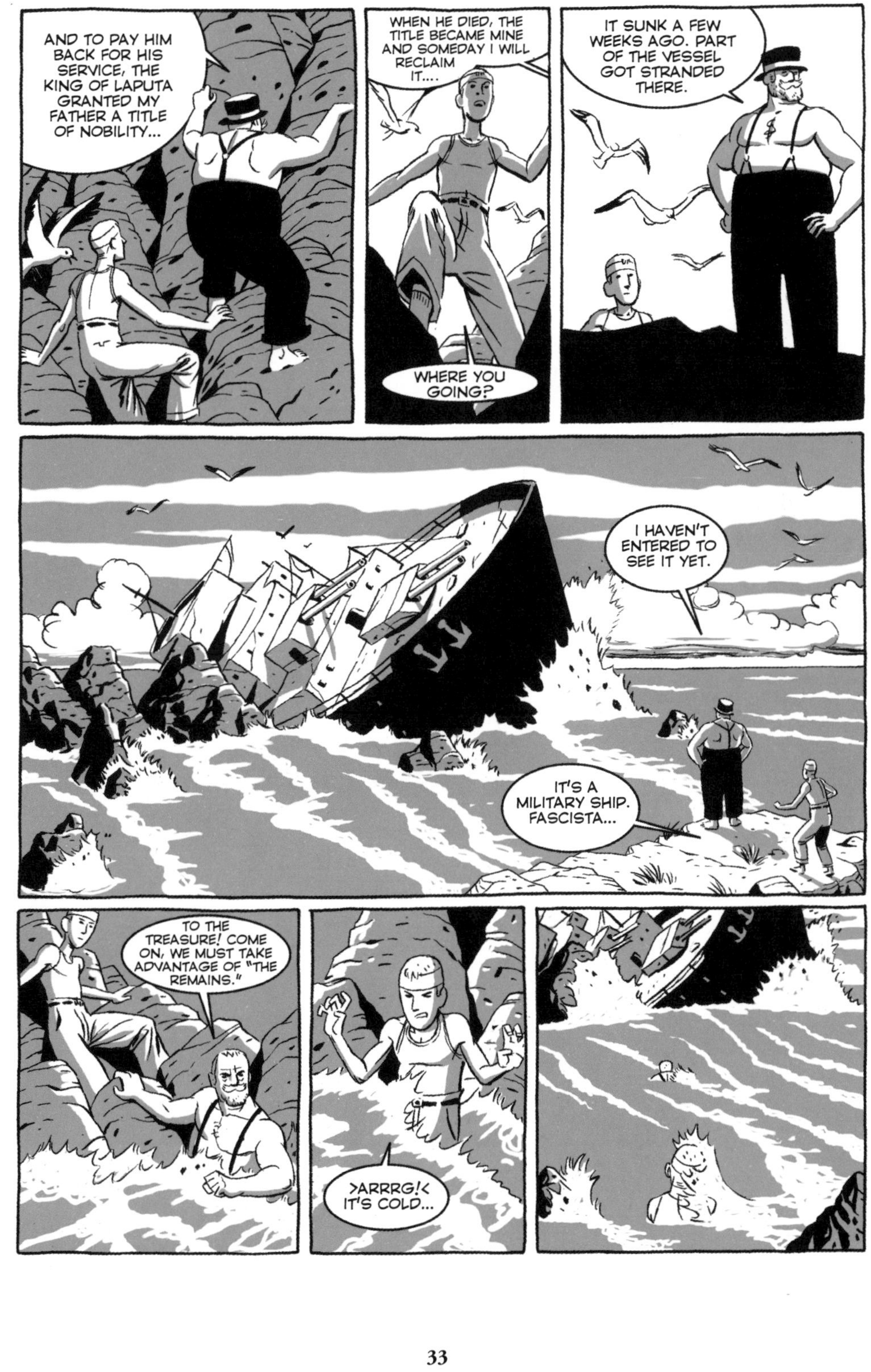
AND TO PAY HIM BACK FOR HIS SERVICE, THE KING OF LAPUTA GRANTED MY FATHER A TITLE OF NOBILITY...
WHEN HE DIED, THE TITLE BECAME MINE AND SOMEDAY I WILL RECLAIM IT....
WHERE YOU GOING?
IT SUNK A FEW WEEKS AGO. PART OF THE VESSEL GOT STRANDED THERE.
I HAVEN'T ENTERED TO SEE IT YET.
IT'S A MILITARY SHIP. FASCISTA...
TO THE TREASURE! COME ON, WE MUST TAKE ADVANTAGE OF "THE REMAINS."
>ARRRG!< IT'S COLD...

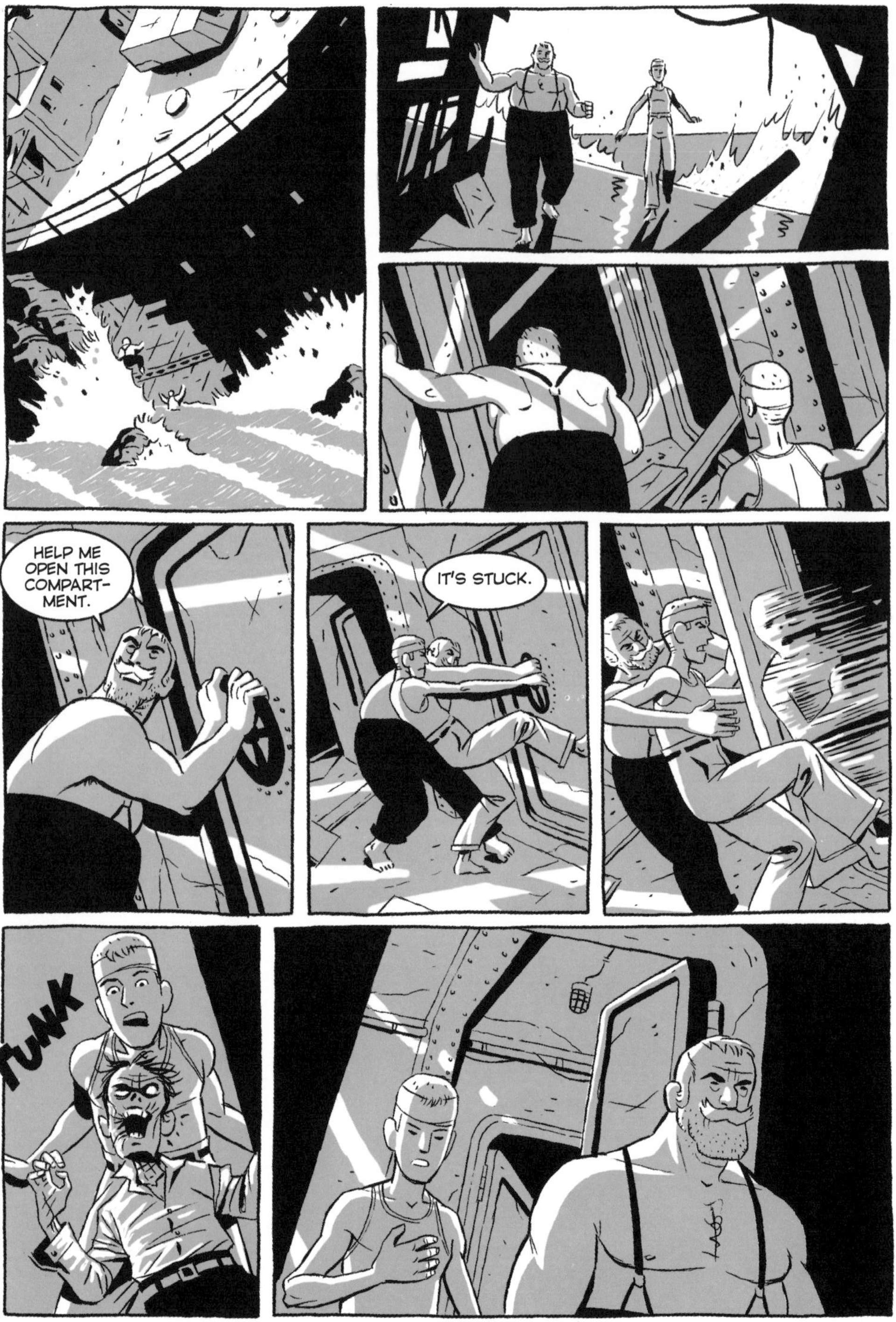
HELP ME OPEN THIS COMPART-MENT.
IT'S STUCK.
TUNK

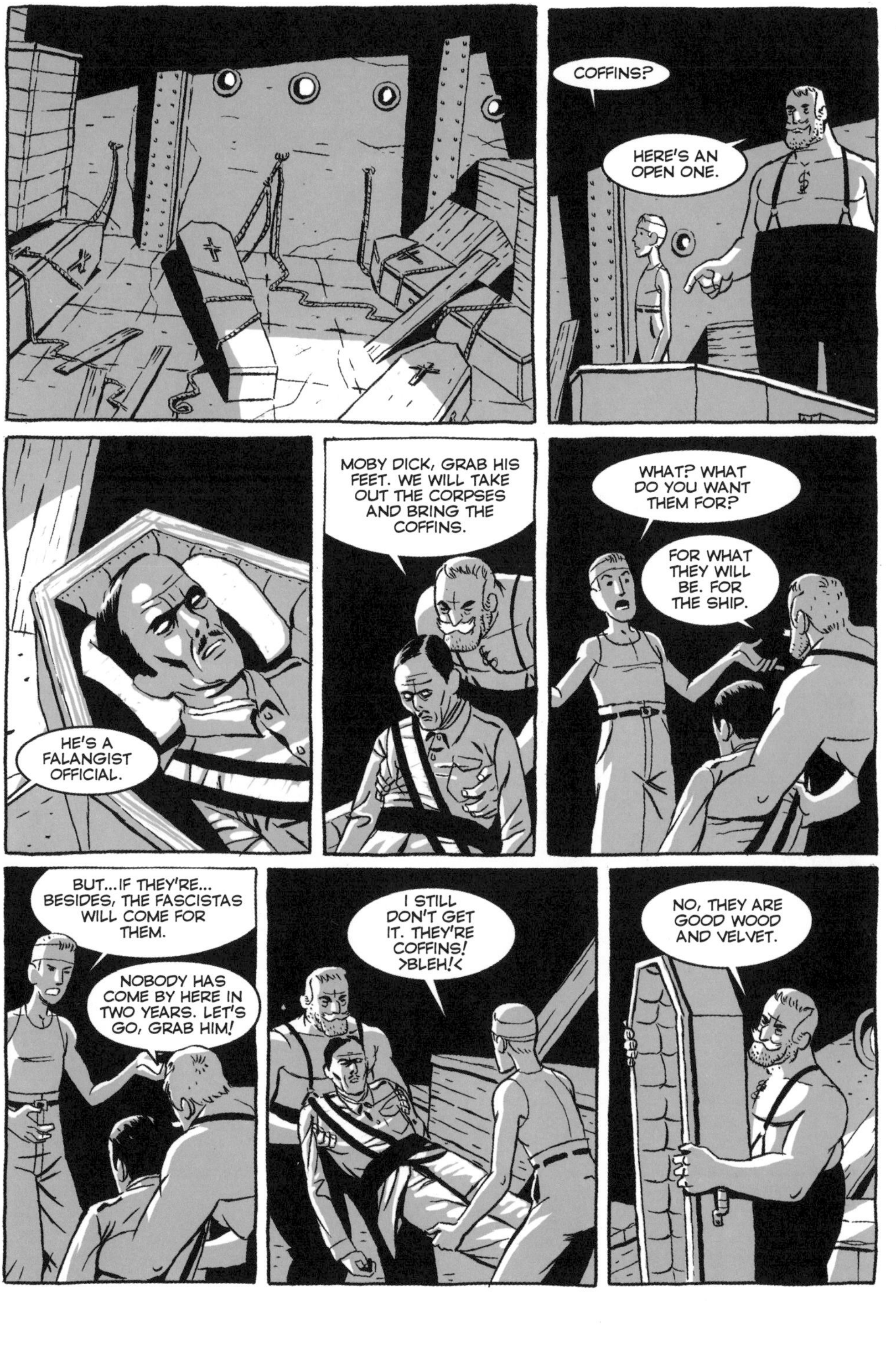
COFFINS?
HERE'S AN OPEN ONE.
HE'S A FALANGIST OFFICIAL.
MOBY DICK, GRAB HIS FEET. WE WILL TAKE OUT THE CORPSES AND BRING THE COFFINS.
WHAT? WHAT DO YOU WANT THEM FOR?
FOR WHAT THEY WILL BE. FOR THE SHIP.
BUT...IF THEY'RE... BESIDES, THE FASCISTAS WILL COME FOR THEM.
NOBODY HAS COME BY HERE IN TWO YEARS. LET'S GO, GRAB HIM!
I STILL DON'T GET IT. THEY'RE COFFINS! >BLEH!<
NO, THEY ARE GOOD WOOD AND VELVET.

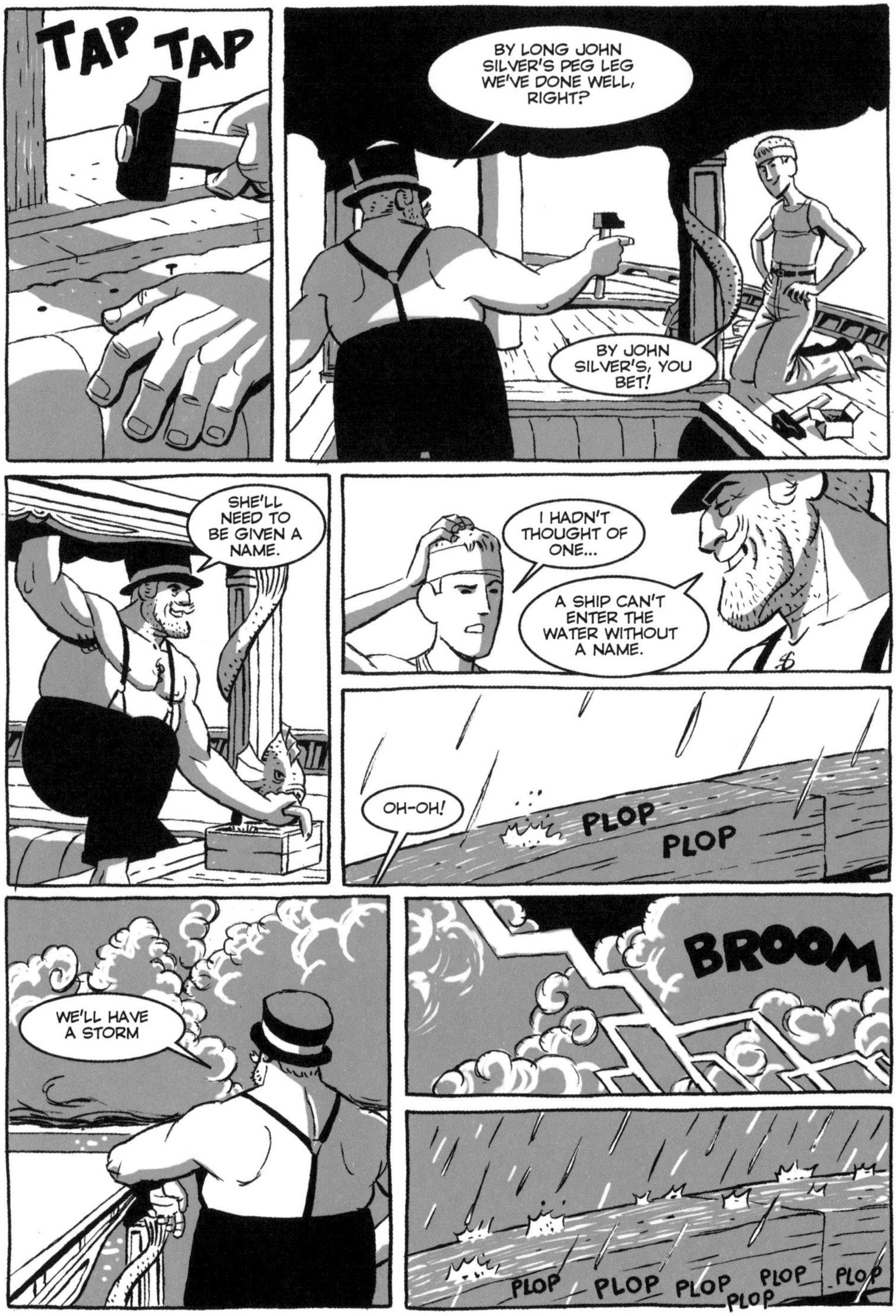
TAP TAP
BY LONG JOHN SILVER'S PEG LEG WE'VE DONE WELL, RIGHT?
BY JOHN SILVER'S, YOU BET!
SHE'LL NEED TO BE GIVEN A NAME.
I HADN'T THOUGHT OF ONE...
A SHIP CAN'T ENTER THE WATER WITHOUT A NAME.
OH-OH!
PLOP
PLOP
WE'LL HAVE A STORM
BROOM
PLOP PLOP PLOP PLOP PLOP PLOP

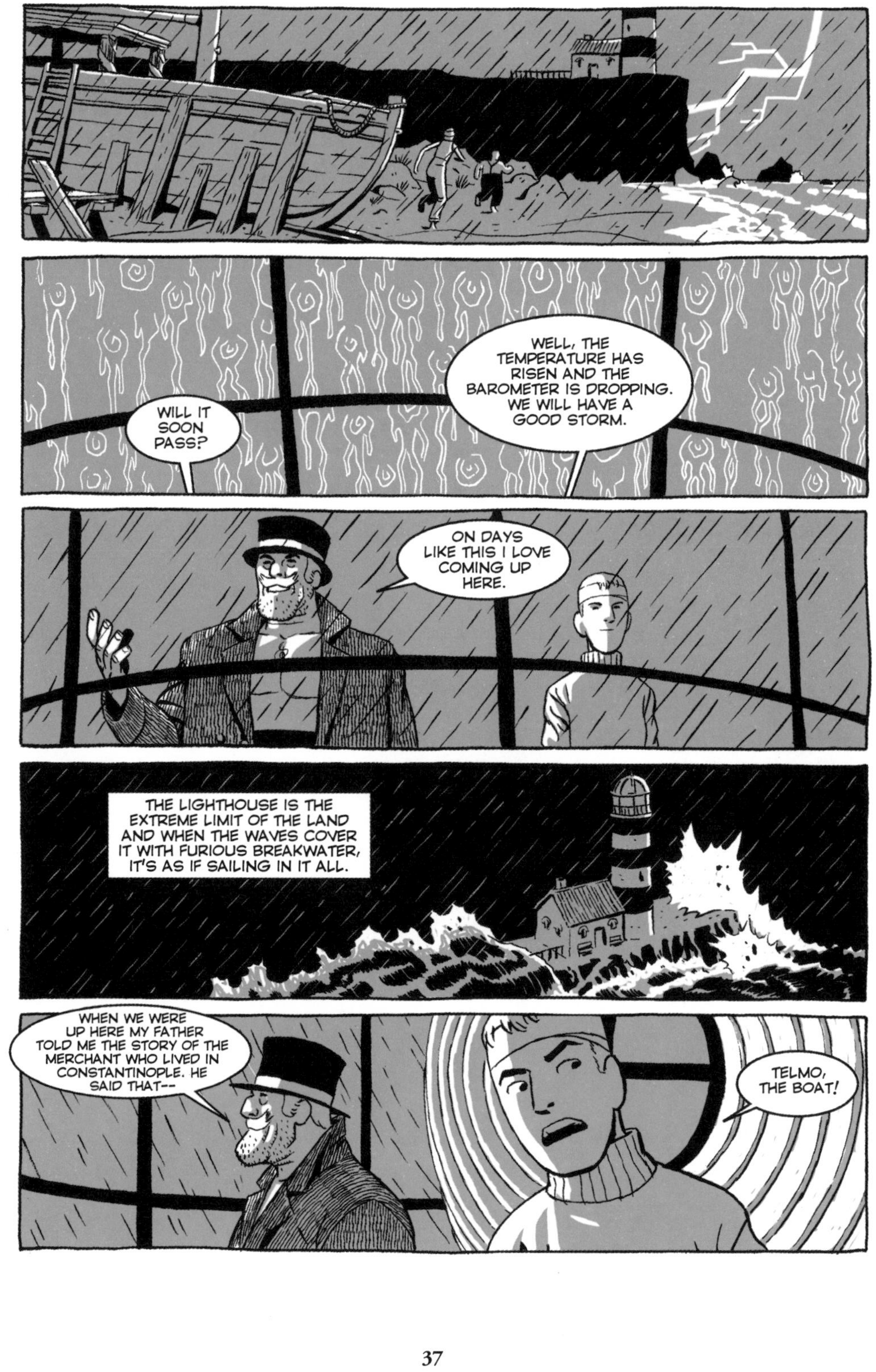

WILL IT SOON PASS?
WELL, THE TEMPERATURE HAS RISEN AND THE BAROMETER IS DROPPING. WE WILL HAVE A GOOD STORM.
ON DAYS LIKE THIS I LOVE COMING UP HERE.
THE LIGHTHOUSE IS THE EXTREME LIMIT OF THE LAND AND WHEN THE WAVES COVER IT WITH FURIOUS BREAKWATER, IT'S AS IF SAILING IN IT ALL.
WHEN WE WERE UP HERE MY FATHER TOLD ME THE STORY OF THE MERCHANT WHO LIVED IN CONSTANTINOPLE. HE SAID THAT--
TELMO, THE BOAT!

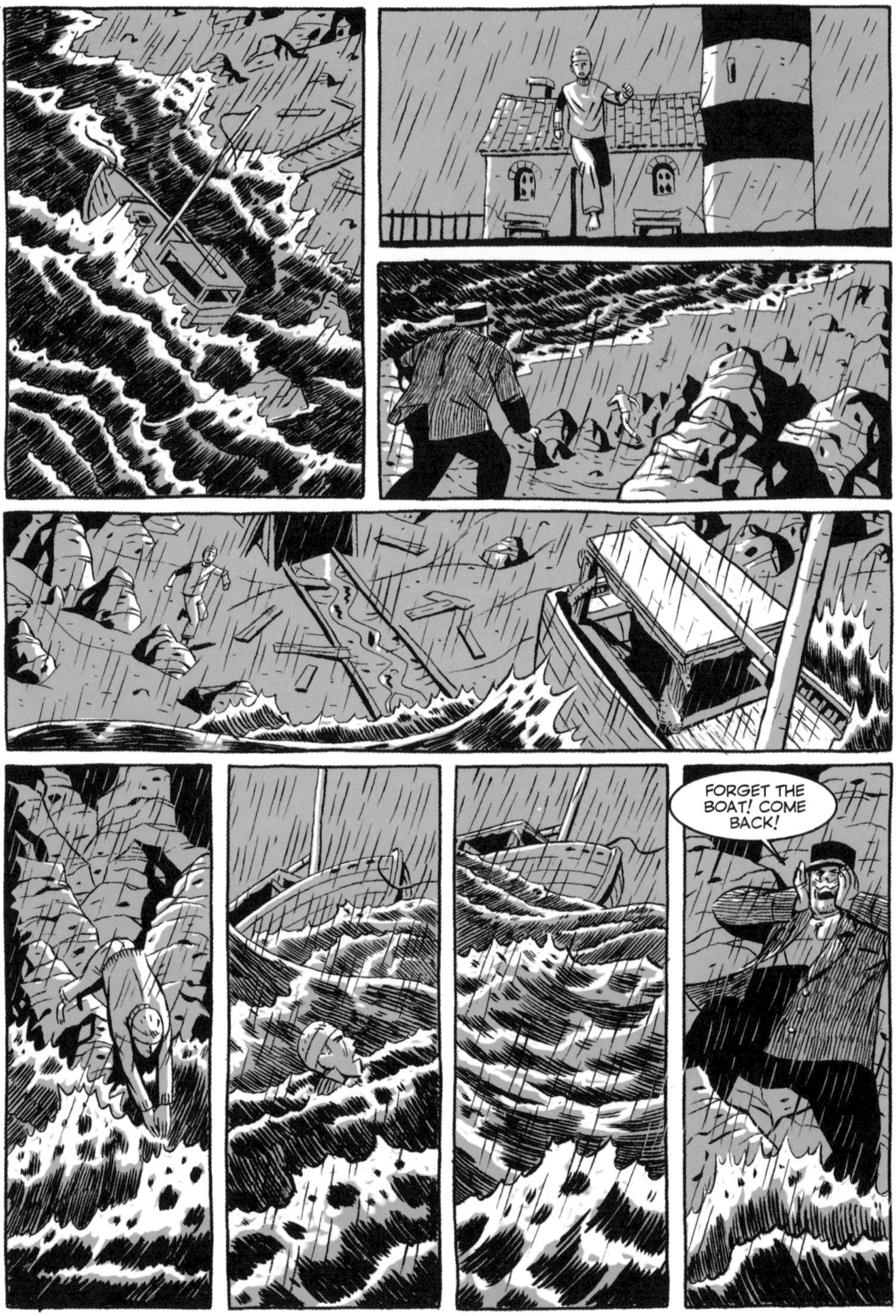
FORGET THE BOAT! COME BACK!

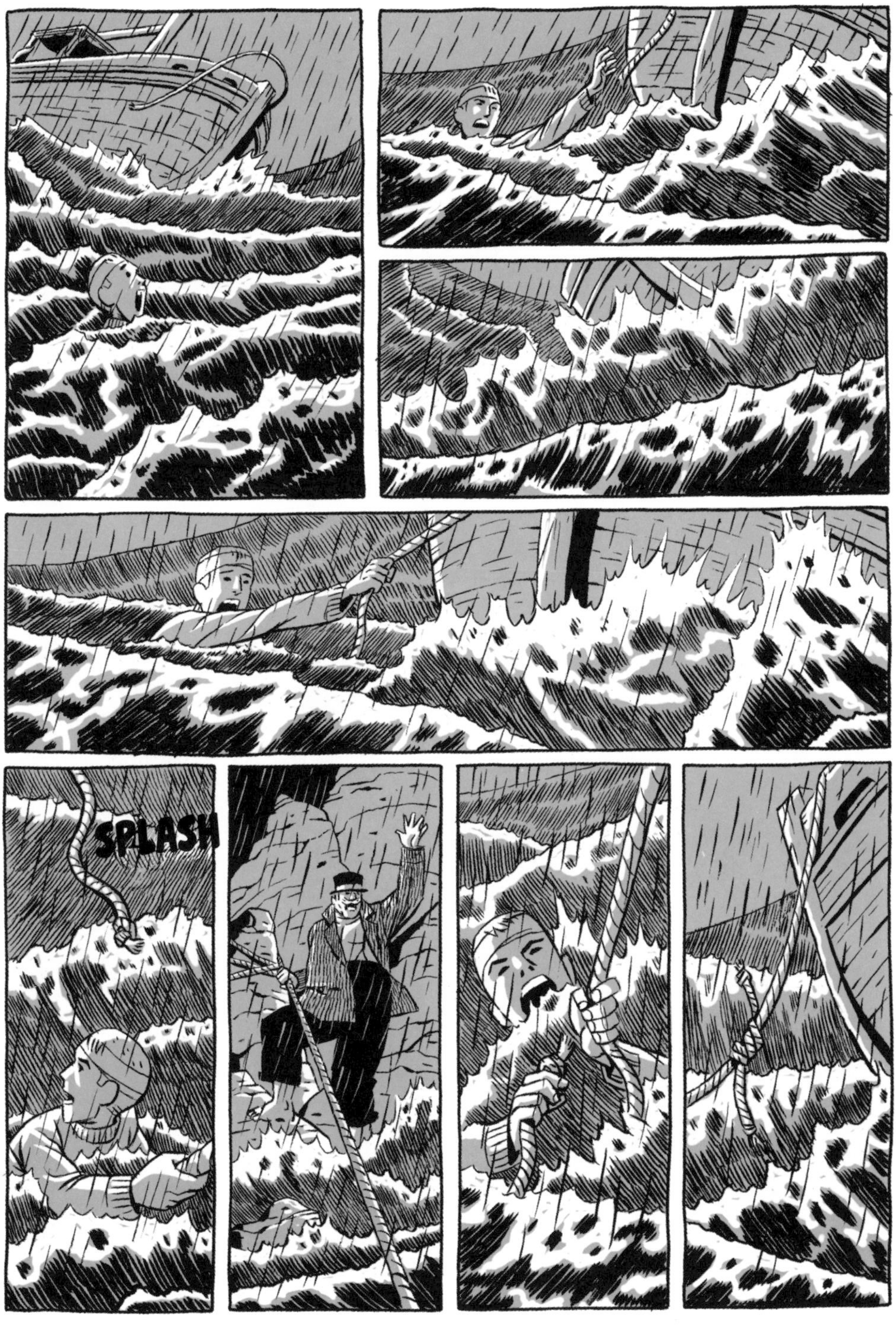
SPLASH

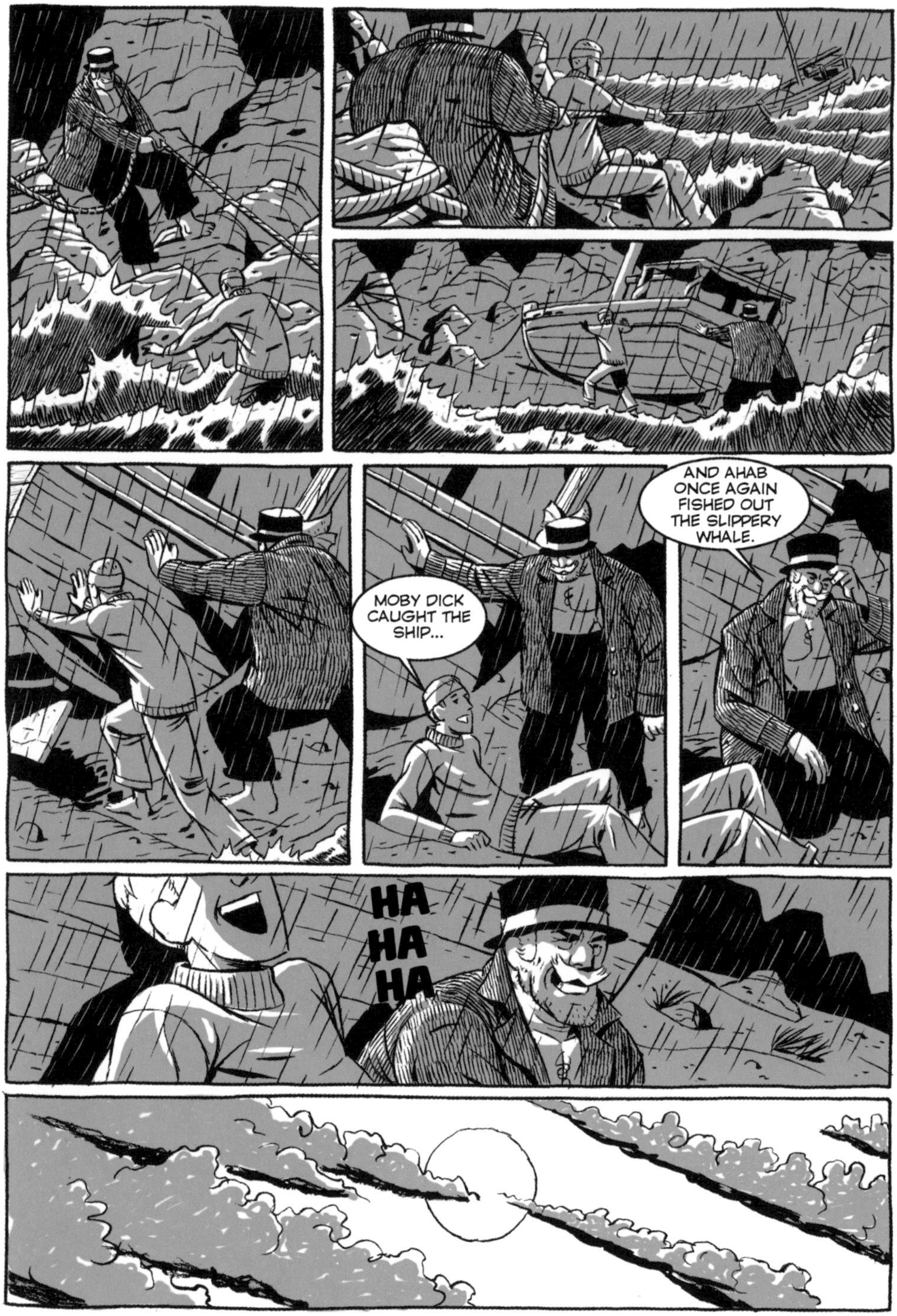
MOBY DICK CAUGHT THE SHIP...
AND AHAB ONCE AGAIN FISHED OUT THE SLIPPERY WHALE.
HA HA HA

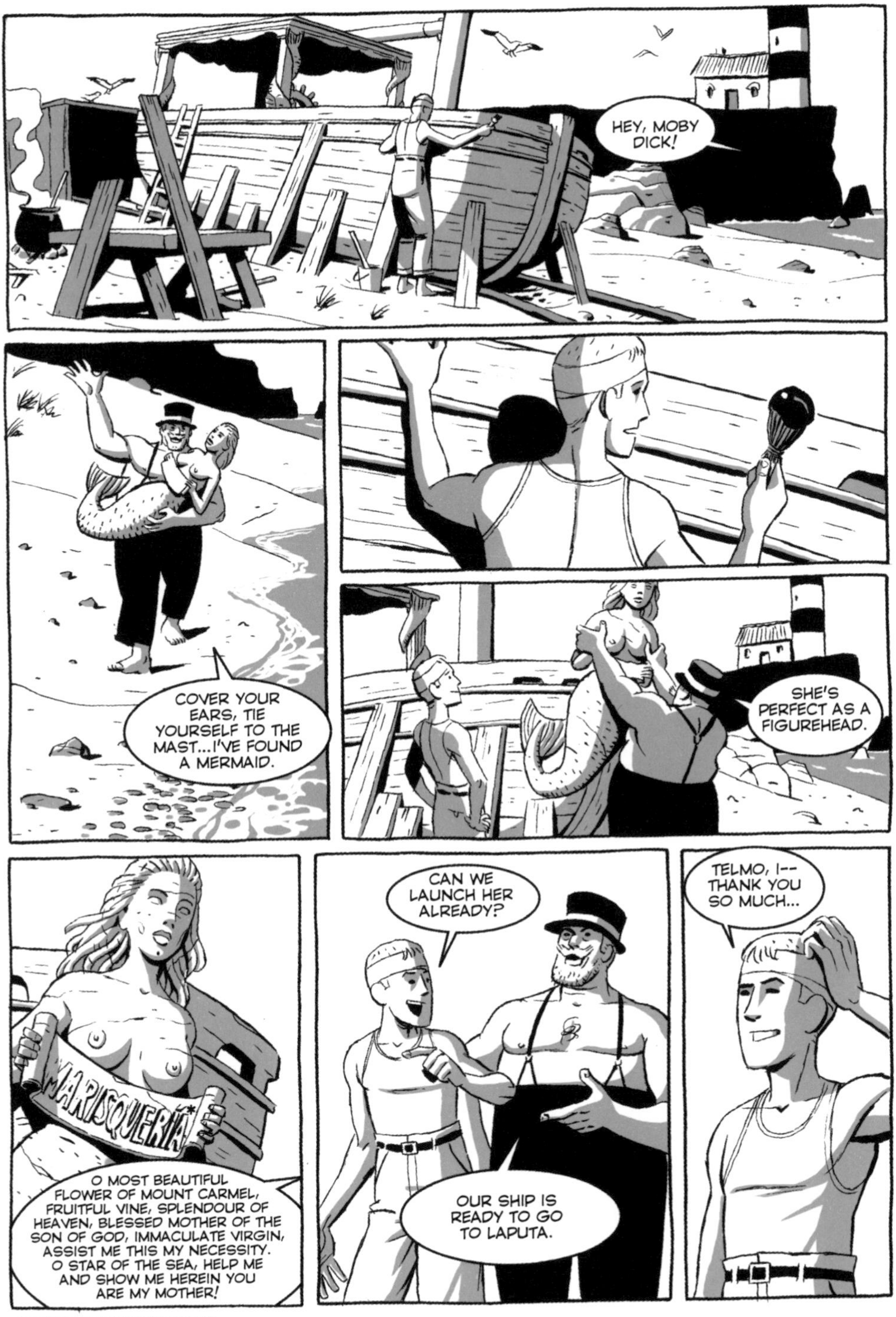
HEY, MOBY DICK!
COVER YOUR EARS, TIE YOURSELF TO THE MAST...I'VE FOUND A MERMAID.
SHE'S PERFECT AS A FIGUREHEAD.
MARISQUERIA*
O MOST BEAUTIFUL FLOWER OF MOUNT CARMEL, FRUITFUL VINE, SPLENDOUR OF HEAVEN, BLESSED MOTHER OF THE SON OF GOD, IMMACULATE VIRGIN, ASSIST ME THIS MY NECESSITY. O STAR OF THE SEA, HELP ME AND SHOW ME HEREIN YOU ARE MY MOTHER!
CAN WE LAUNCH HER ALREADY?
OUR SHIP IS READY TO GO TO LAPUTA.
TELMO, I-- THANK YOU SO MUCH...

*SEAFOOD RESTAURANT

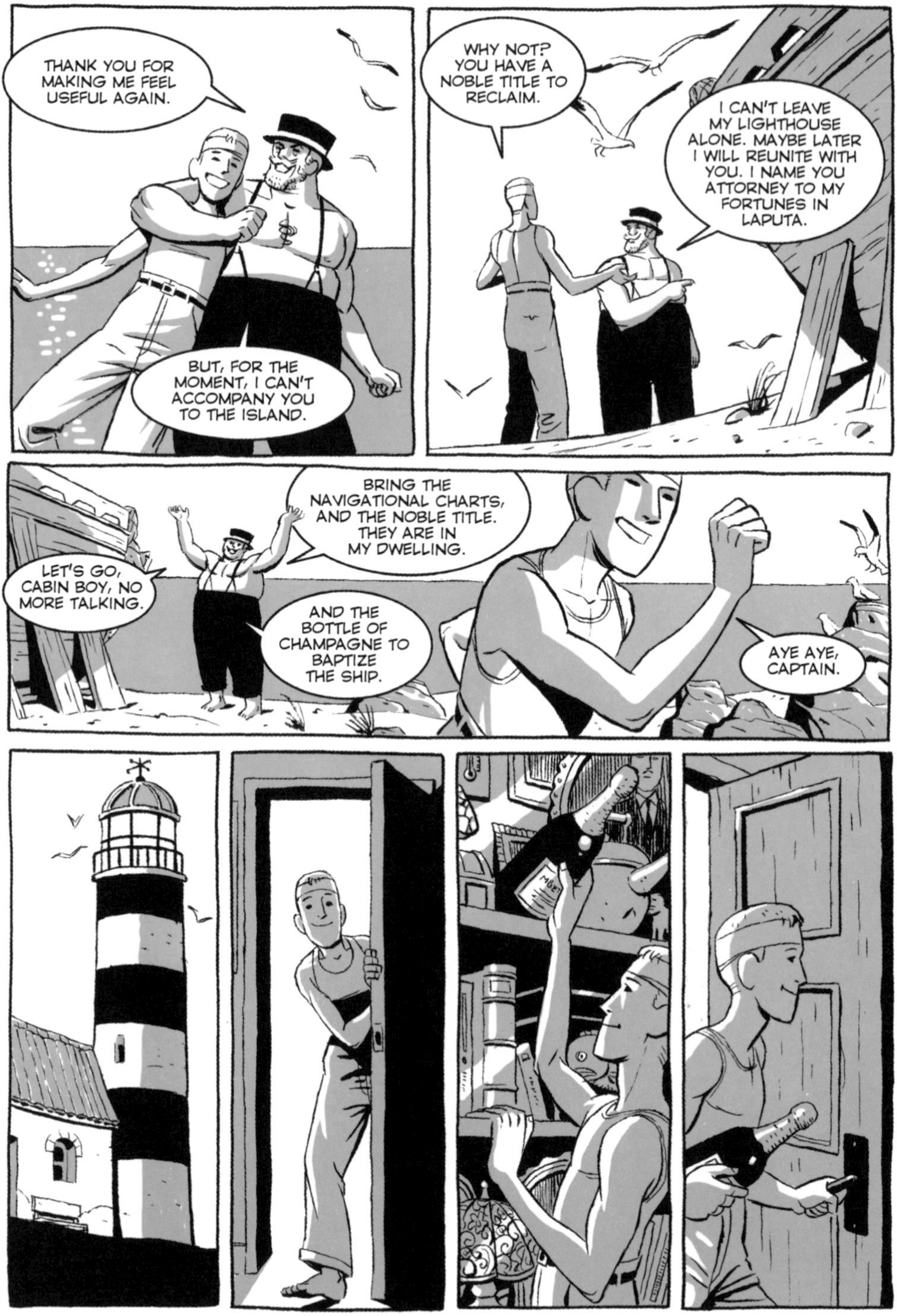
THANK YOU FOR MAKING ME FEEL USEFUL AGAIN.
BUT, FOR THE MOMENT, I CAN'T ACCOMPANY YOU TO THE ISLAND.
WHY NOT? YOU HAVE A NOBLE TITLE TO RECLAIM.
I CAN'T LEAVE MY LIGHTHOUSE ALONE. MAYBE LATER I WILL REUNITE WITH YOU. I NAME YOU ATTORNEY TO MY FORTUNES IN LAPUTA.
LET'S GO, CABIN BOY, NO MORE TALKING.
BRING THE NAVIGATIONAL CHARTS, AND THE NOBLE TITLE. THEY ARE IN MY DWELLING.
AND THE BOTTLE OF CHAMPAGNE TO BAPTIZE THE SHIP.
AYE AYE, CAPTAIN.

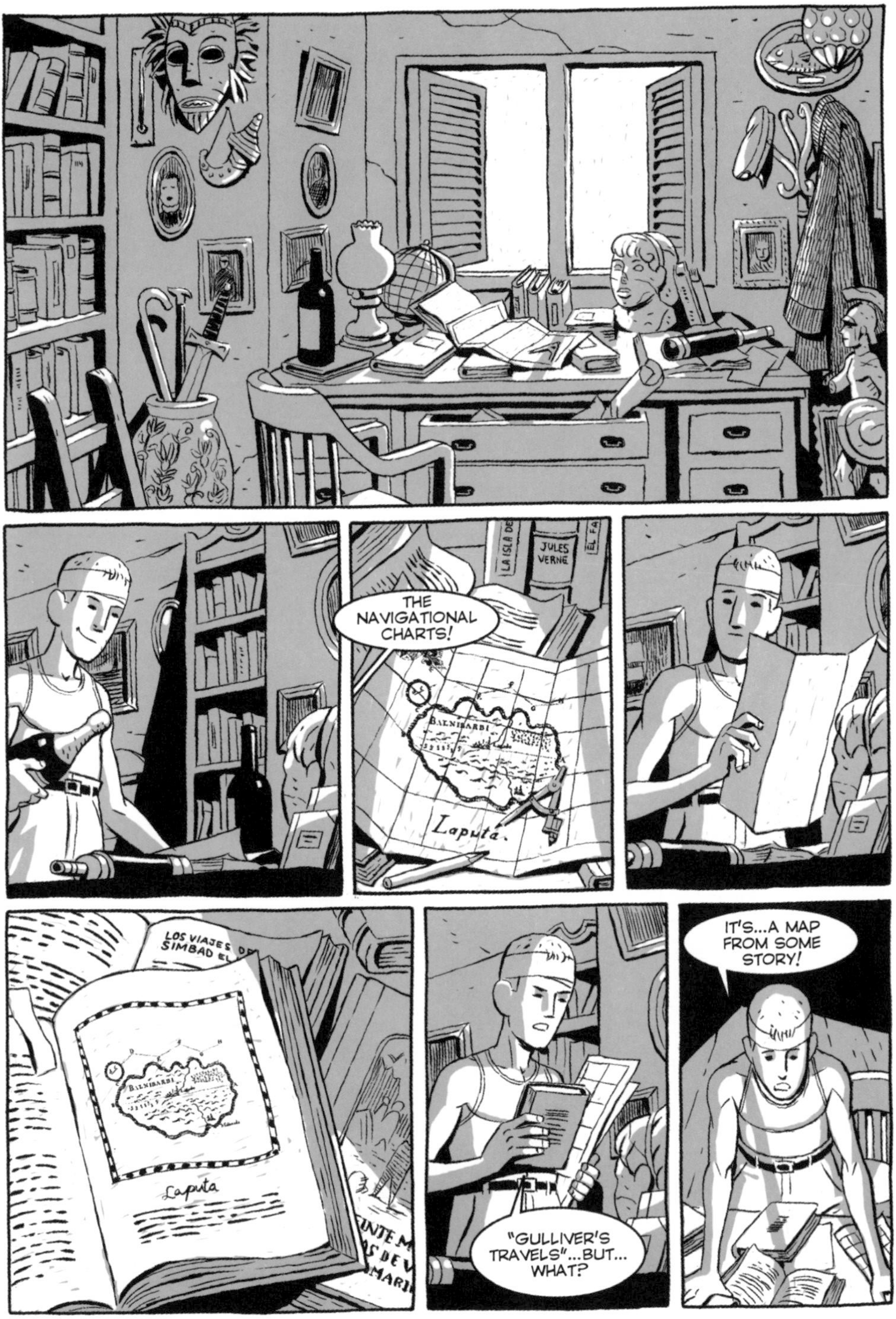
LA ISLA DE
JULES VERNE
EL FA
THE NAVIGATIONAL CHARTS!
BALNIBARBI
Laputa
LOS VIAJES DE
SIMBAD EL
BALNIBARBI
Laputa
"GULLIVER'S TRAVELS"...BUT... WHAT?
IT'S...A MAP FROM SOME STORY!

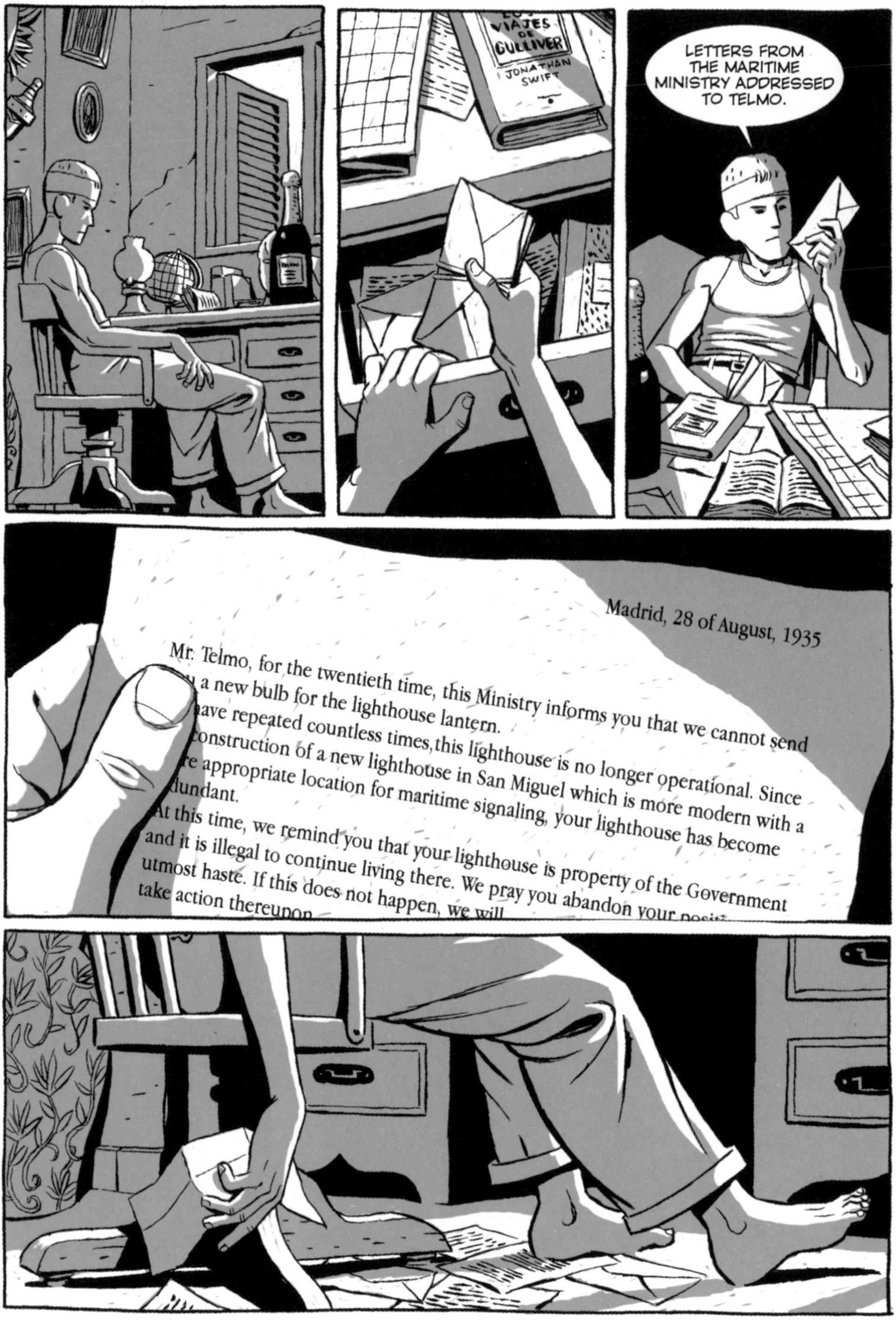
VIAJES
DE
GULLIVER
JONATHAN
SWIFT
LETTERS FROM THE MARITIME MINISTRY ADDRESSED TO TELMO.
Madrid, 28 of August, 1935
Mr. Telmo, for the twentieth time, this Ministry informs you that we cannot send
a new bulb for the lighthouse lantern.
ave repeated countless times, this lighthouse is no longer operational. Since
onstruction of a new lighthouse in San Miguel which is more modern with a
e appropriate location for maritime signaling, your lighthouse has become
dundant.
At this time, we remind you that your lighthouse is property of the Government
and it is illegal to continue living there. We pray you abandon your
utmost haste. If this does not happen, we will
take action thereupon

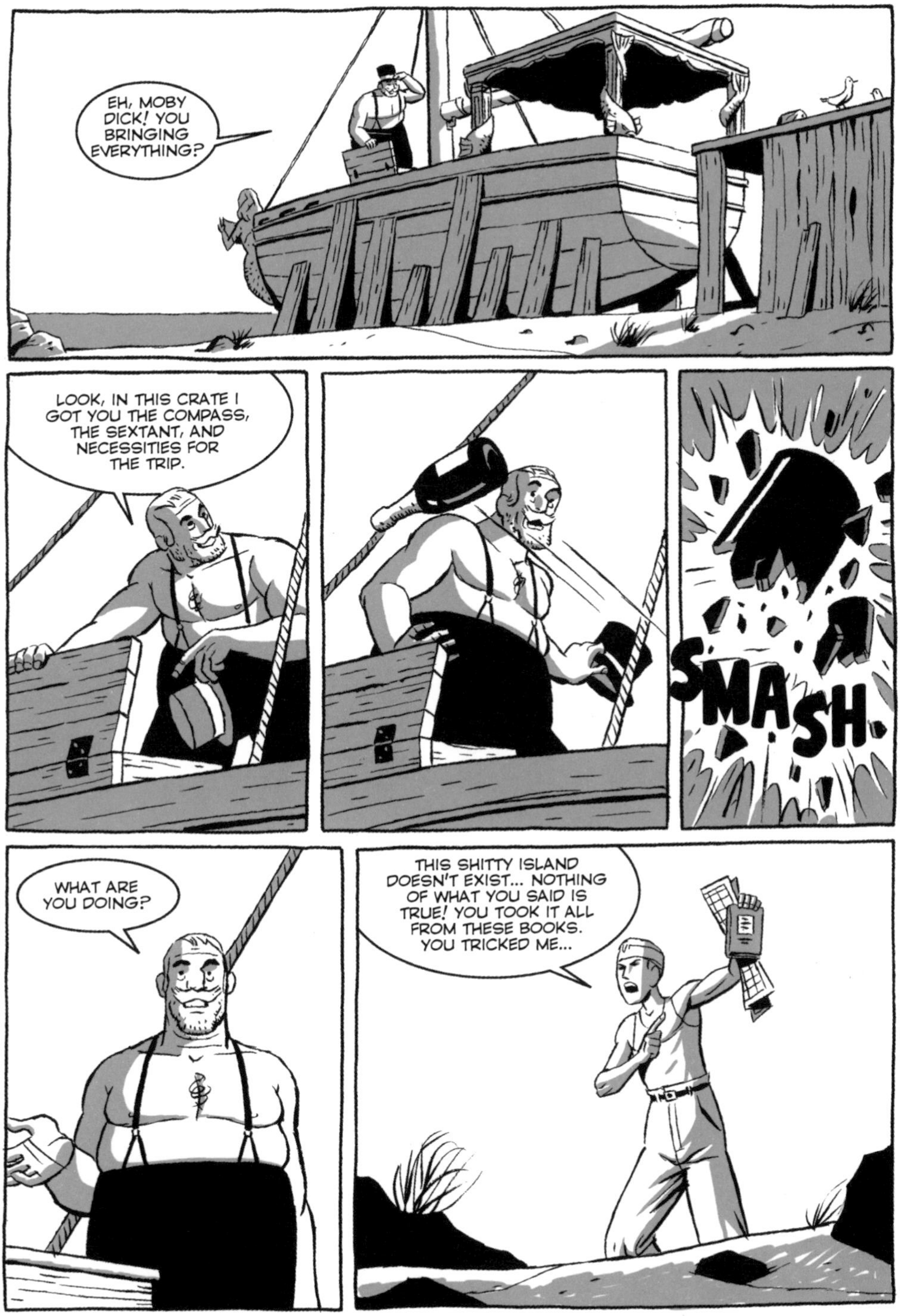
EH, MOBY DICK! YOU BRINGING EVERYTHING?
LOOK, IN THIS CRATE I GOT YOU THE COMPASS, THE SEXTANT, AND NECESSITIES FOR THE TRIP.
SMASH.
WHAT ARE YOU DOING?
THIS SHITTY ISLAND DOESN'T EXIST... NOTHING OF WHAT YOU SAID IS TRUE! YOU TOOK IT ALL FROM THESE BOOKS. YOU TRICKED ME...

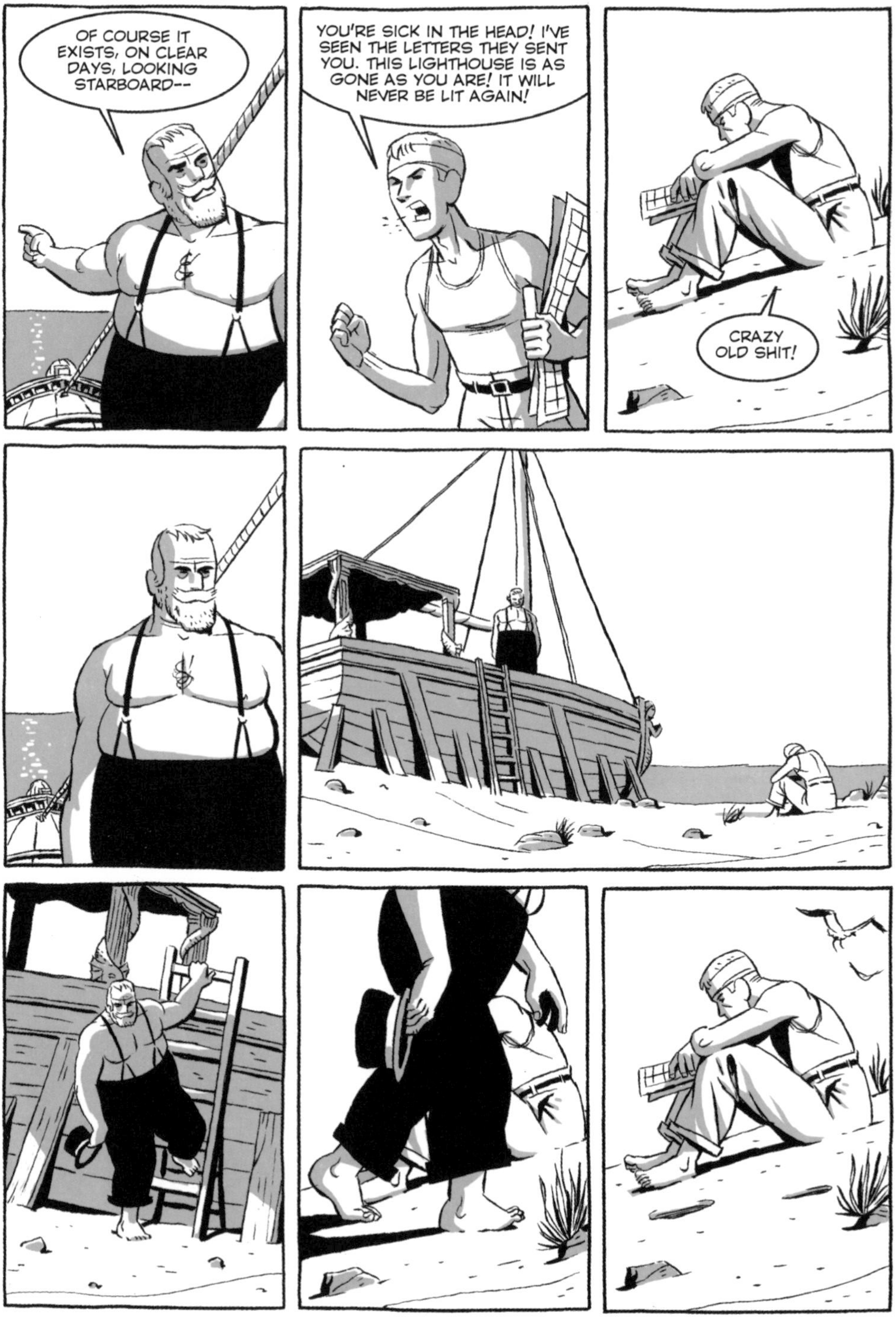
OF COURSE IT EXISTS, ON CLEAR DAYS, LOOKING STARBOARD--
YOU'RE SICK IN THE HEAD! I'VE SEEN THE LETTERS THEY SENT YOU. THIS LIGHTHOUSE IS AS GONE AS YOU ARE! IT WILL NEVER BE LIT AGAIN!
CRAZY OLD SHIT!

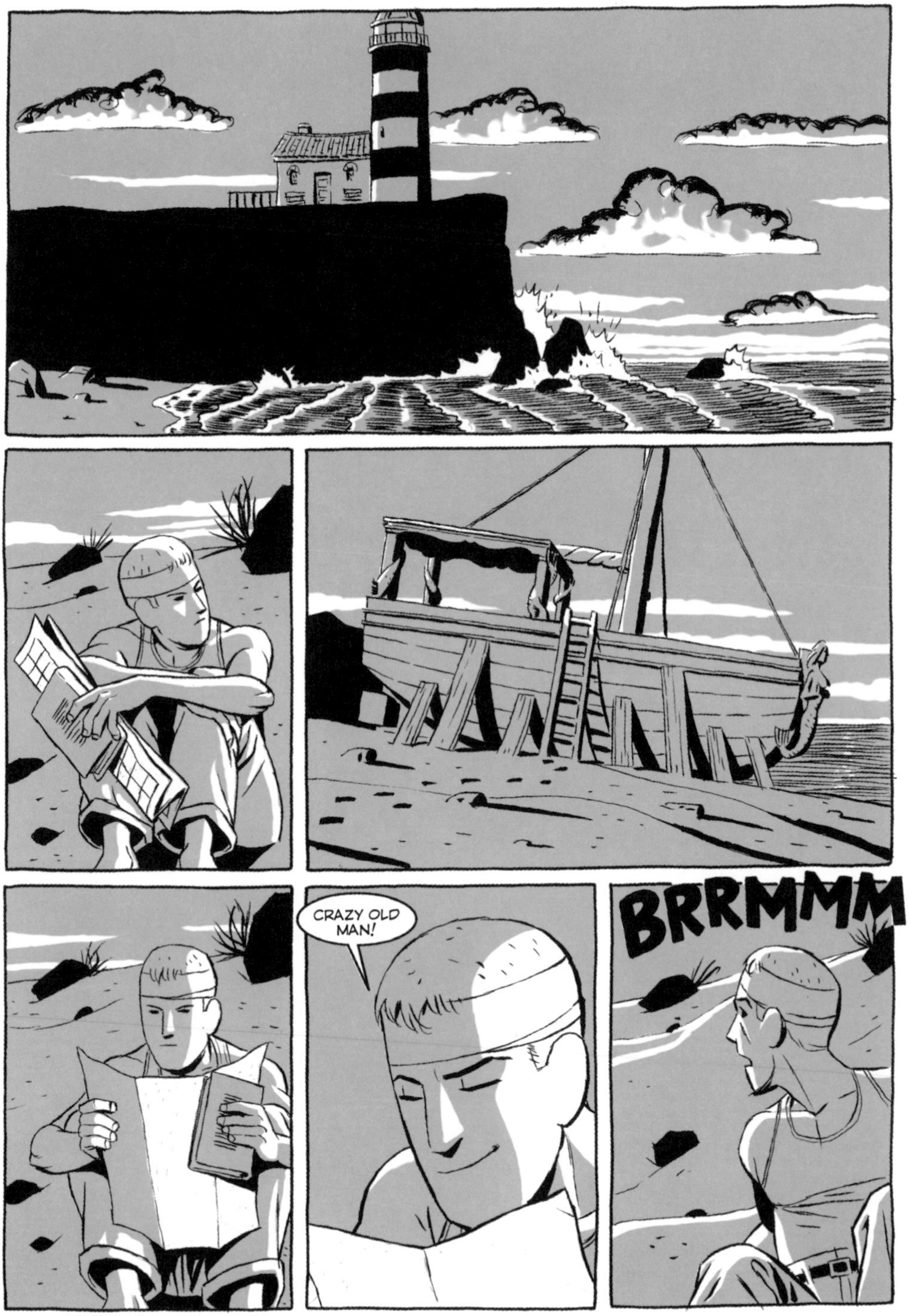
CRAZY OLD MAN!
BRRMMM

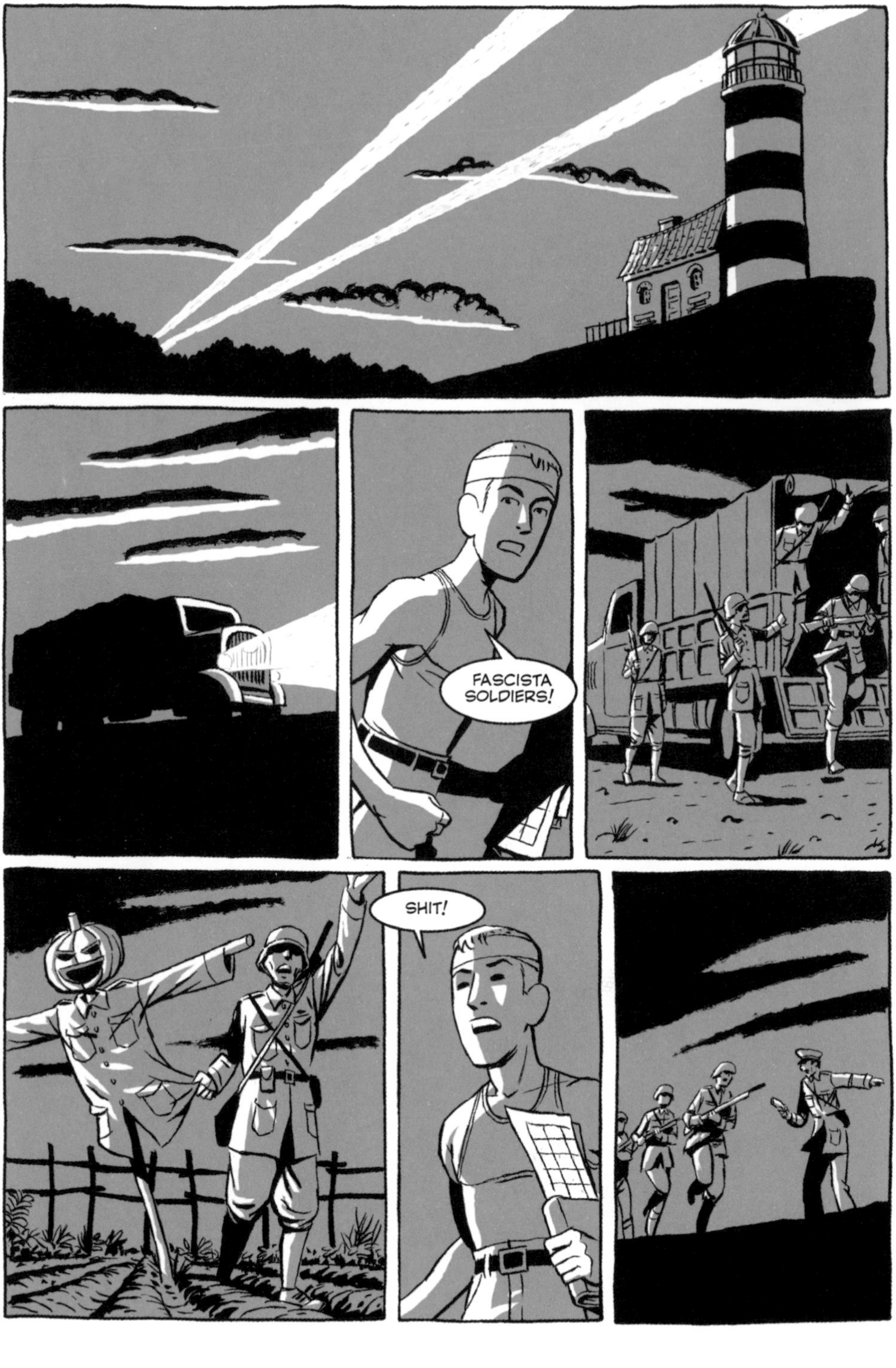
FASCISTA SOLDIERS!
SHIT!

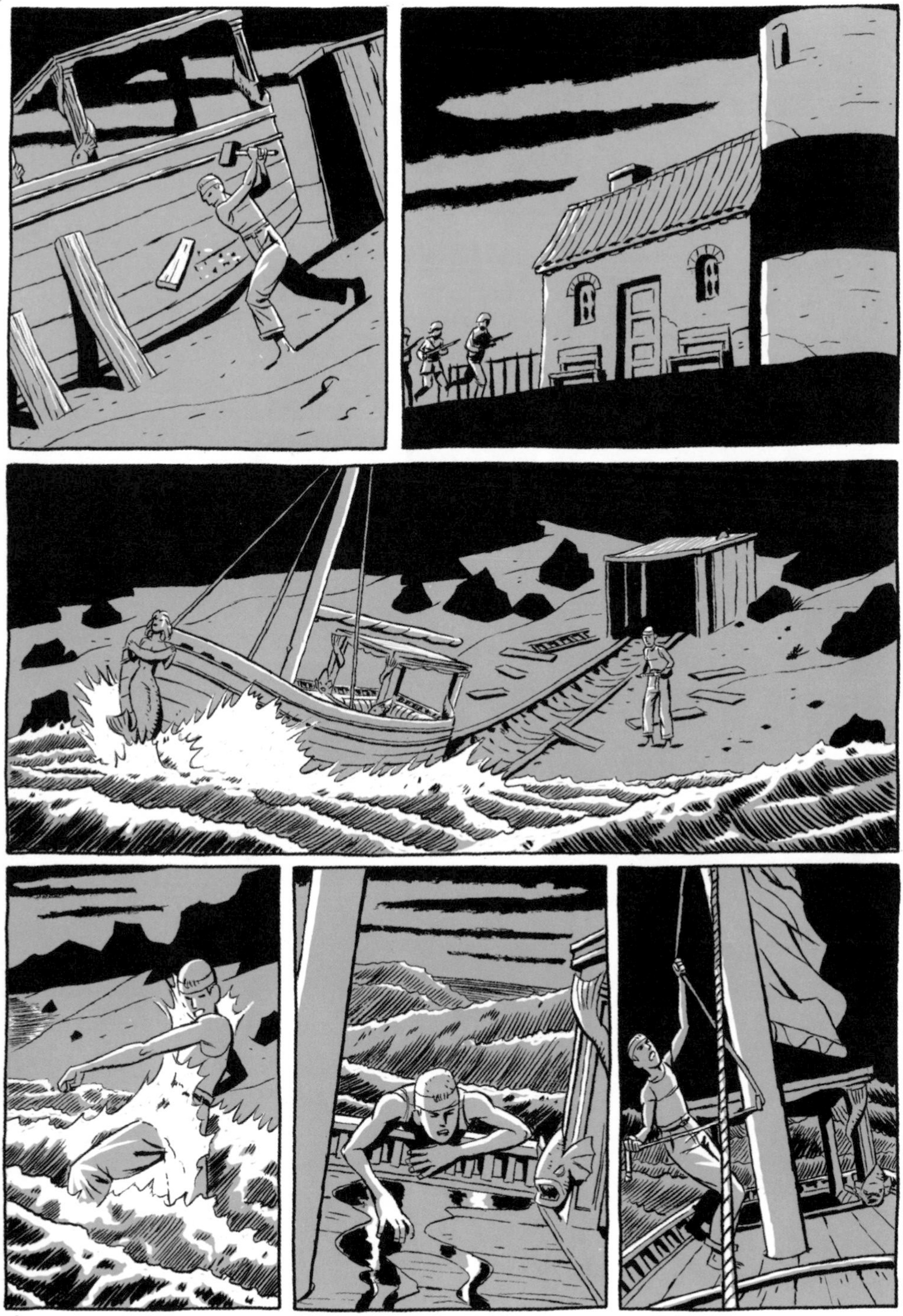

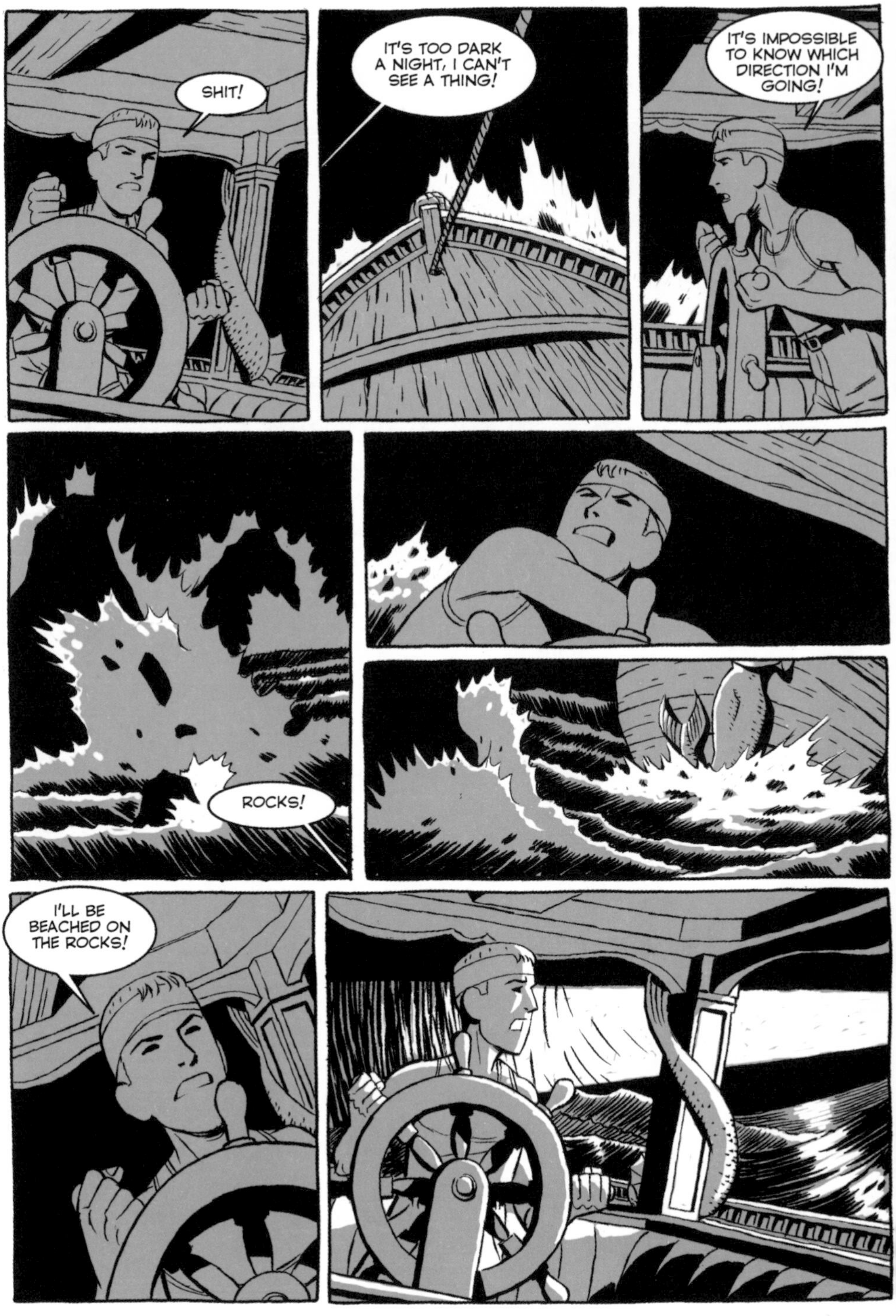
SHIT!
IT'S TOO DARK A NIGHT, I CAN'T SEE A THING!
IT'S IMPOSSIBLE TO KNOW WHICH DIRECTION I'M GOING!
ROCKS!
I'LL BE BEACHED ON THE ROCKS!

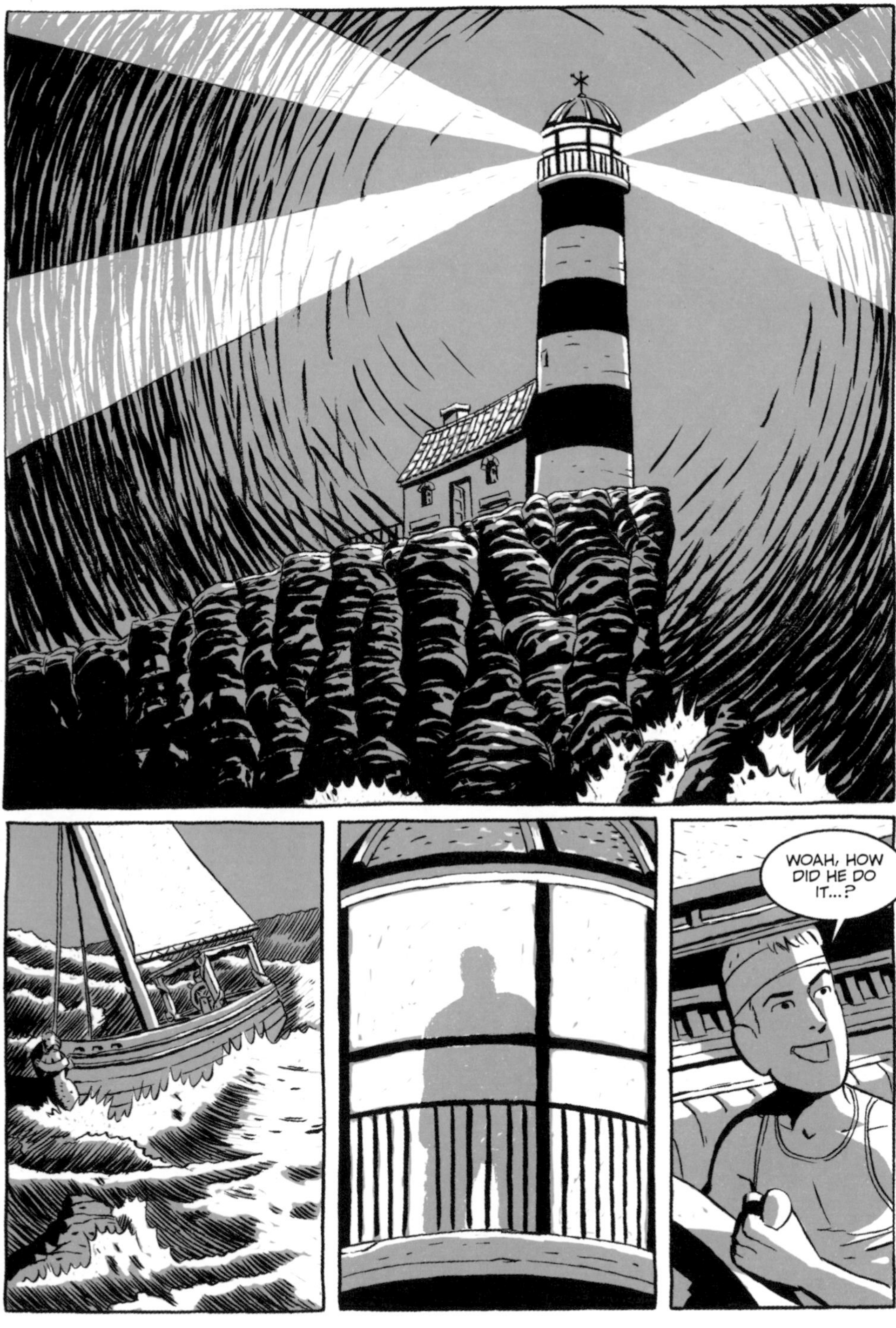
WOAH, HOW DID HE DO IT...?

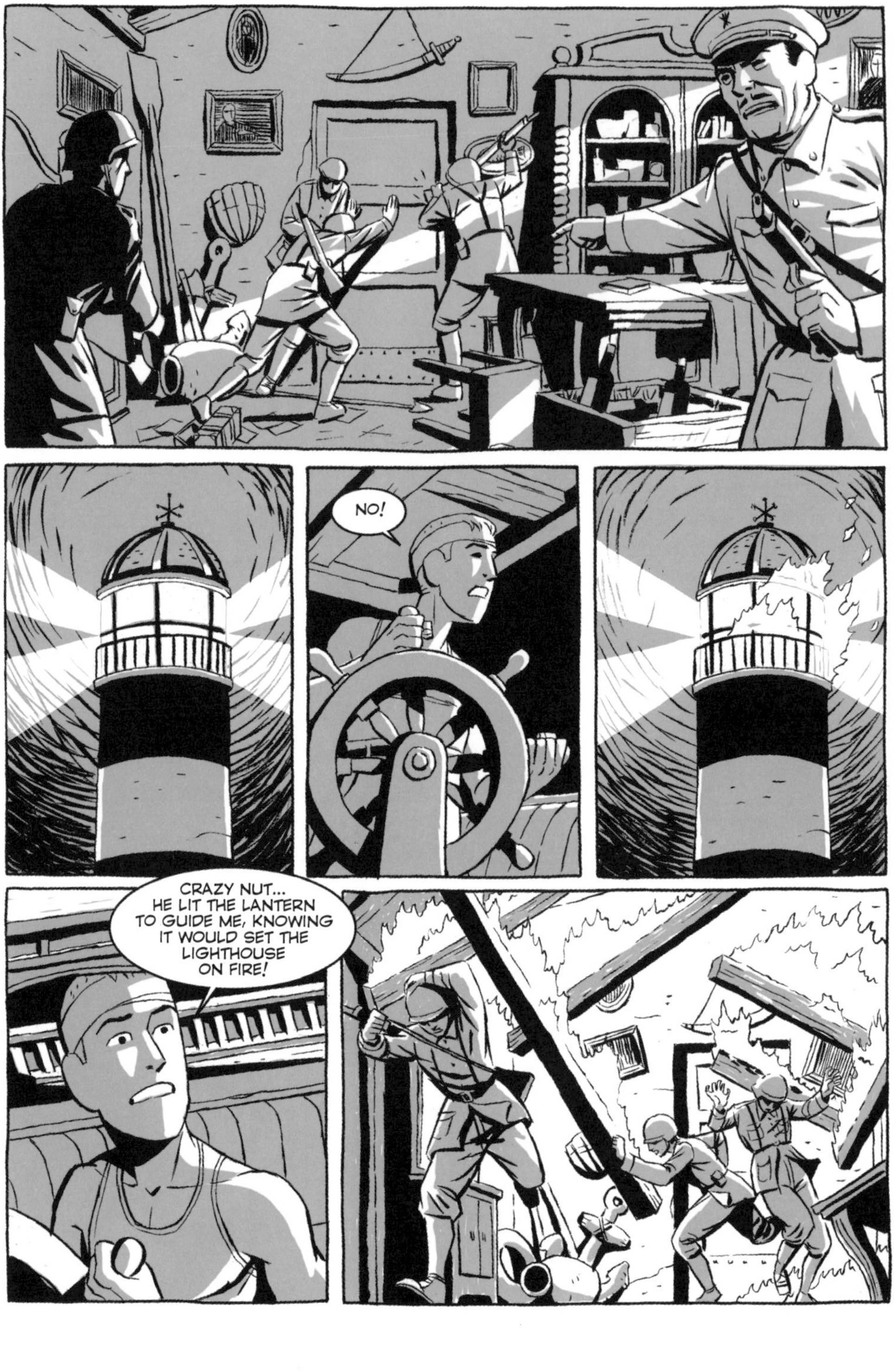
NO!
CRAZY NUT... HE LIT THE LANTERN TO GUIDE ME, KNOWING IT WOULD SET THE LIGHTHOUSE ON FIRE!

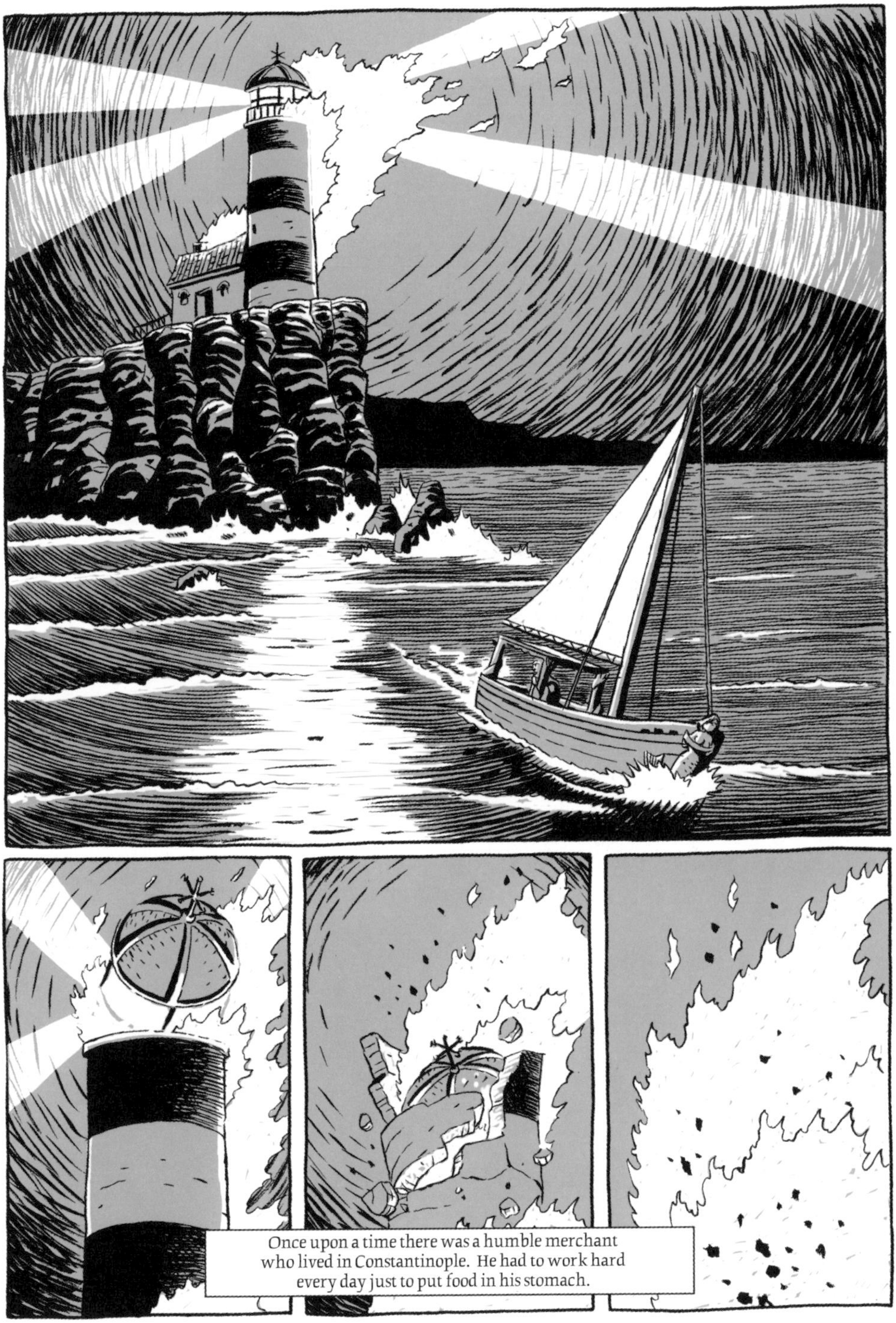
Once upon a time there was a humble merchant who lived in Constantinople. He had to work hard every day just to put food in his stomach.

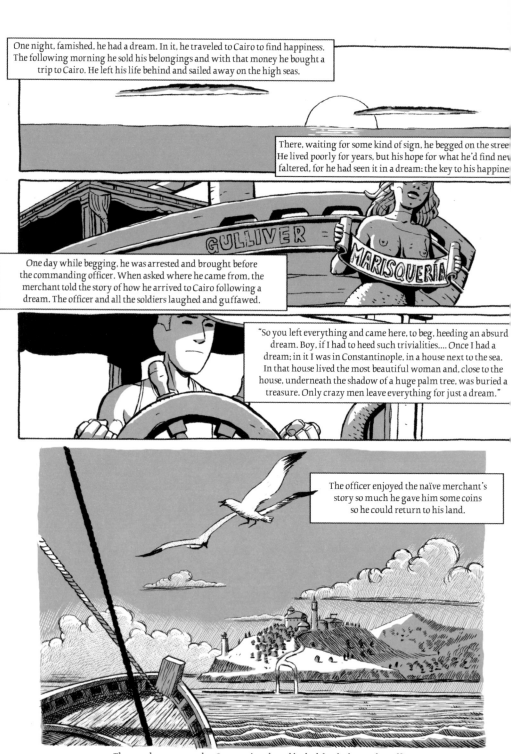

One night, famished, he had a dream. In it, he traveled to Cairo to find happiness. The following morning he sold his belongings and with that money he bought a trip to Cairo. He left his life behind and sailed away on the high seas.

There, waiting for some kind of sign, he begged on the stree[t]. He lived poorly for years, but his hope for what he'd find nev[er] faltered, for he had seen it in a dream: the key to his happine[ss].

One day while begging, he was arrested and brought before the commanding officer. When asked where he came from, the merchant told the story of how he arrived to Cairo following a dream. The officer and all the soldiers laughed and guffawed.

"So you left everything and came here, to beg, heeding an absurd dream. Boy, if I had to heed such trivialities.... Once I had a dream; in it I was in Constantinople, in a house next to the sea. In that house lived the most beautiful woman and, close to the house, underneath the shadow of a huge palm tree, was buried a treasure. Only crazy men leave everything for just a dream."

The officer enjoyed the naïve merchant's story so much he gave him some coins so he could return to his land.

The merchant returned to Constantinople and looked for the house that officer mentioned. There he found the most beautiful woman with whom he married. And near the house, underneath the shadow of an enormous palm tree, he dug up the treasure.

54

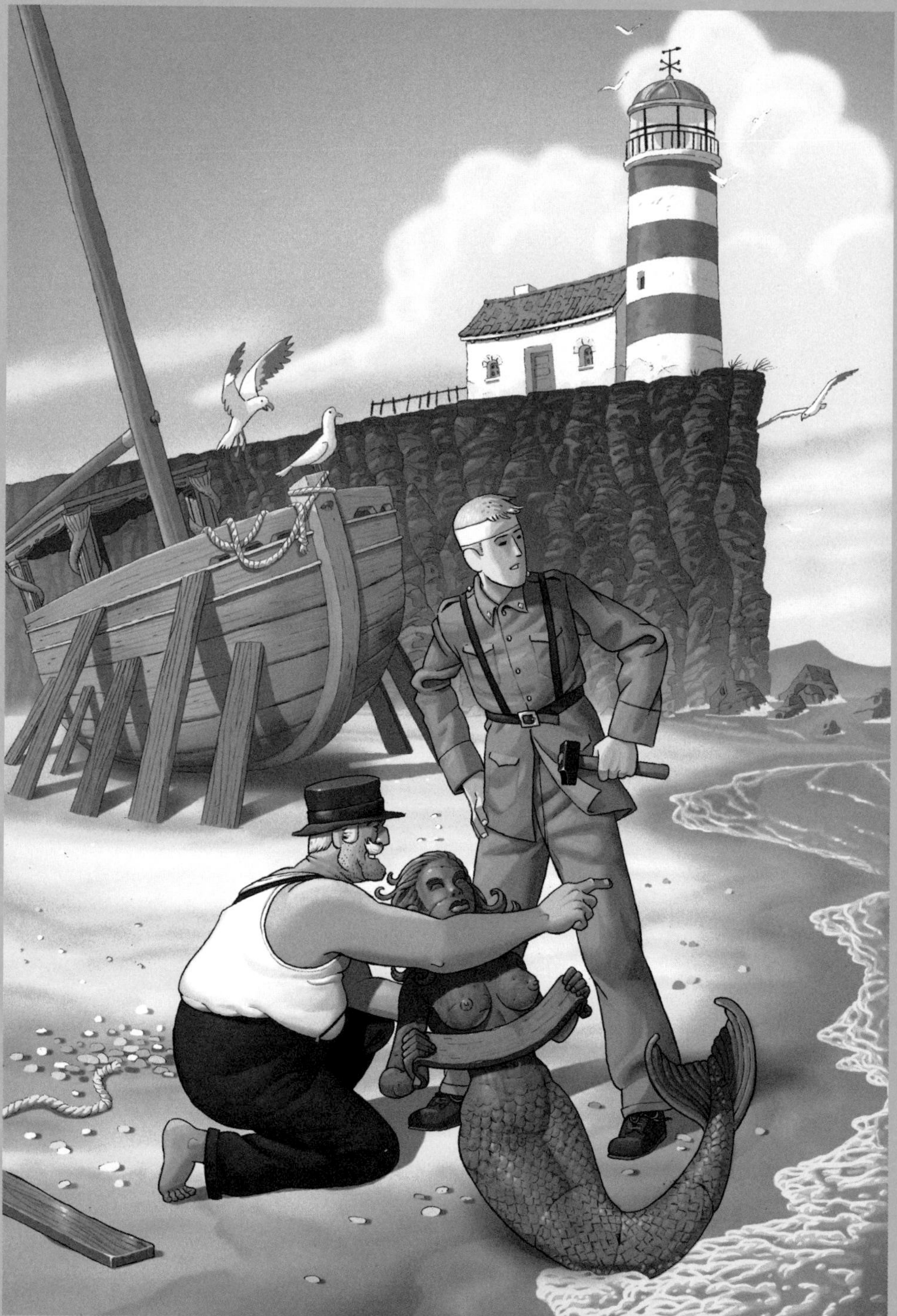

The Eternal Rewrite

One of the happiest and most satisfying moments for an author is when an editor calls to tell you that one of your books will have a new edition. Below your calm and professional tone of voice, you try to hide your childish excitement at the news. But as soon as you hang up the phone begins the difficult dilemma of what, and to what point, do you change the original work, especially if some time has passed since its first edition. There are always aspects that don't please you, dialogue that screeches and scenes that with the passing of time you would have sprouted in a different way.

Practically all the new editions or the translations that other countries have done with my books are different between themselves, even if it is just by a tiny detail. I can't avoid it. It's the same as my mother not being able to resist fussing over her children's hair every time they leave the house. The frequency of the departures or the distance you would be going did not matter. Even if it was just to ask the neighbors something, my mom would comb your hair before leaving. Maybe I have inherited this from her and I can't let an album go out the door without having combed it a bit before. What would the readers say…?

Illustration for the cover of the original Spanish edition (opposite page) and study for same (above).

The French edition of *El Juego Lúgubre* was colored from the black and white original version published by La Cúpula [in Spain]. For a later Spanish edition by Dolmen, I utilized the French edition, where I then changed some dialogue, a bit of the cover page and a face in some panels that would always bother me when I saw it.

Four years passed before *Hijos de la Alhambra* was published in Spain and Italy, so there was the opportunity to correct all that I didn't like. I changed a panel that didn't make sense and I amplified others to make the story a bit more dynamic. I also made changes to the dialogue, modifying them a lot. The capacity to substantially change a story and tie up loose ends by changing just the dialogue, is a possibility in postproduction of a graphic novel. I usually do these before handing in the book.

In *Wrinkles* (Fantagraphics) there were also changes between the French edition and the Spanish one. I had to "Frenchify" some things like the classroom of Emilio, adapt the clocks to the French schedules, and change the menu in Nochebuena. For the Spanish edition, I recuperated the original version. I also added a dialogue on the final page between Esteban and the dog to drive home the sensation of solitude. This last change I added to the second French edition. And the second Spanish edition has a small change of text in respect to the first one.

And also in *Las Calles de Arena,* the Spanish edition is distinct from the French in its translation of some signs, and the second Spanish edition differentiates itself from the first in a detail on the cover image, in the paper stock, and a small text change. With so much change and changing again from one edition to the other and from one language to another, I create a big mess that always stresses me out as, at any time, I could send the wrong version to press.

The Lighthouse is no exception. The French version was printed without the last minute modifications that I made before handing the original work in to my Spanish publisher Astiberri. Proof of this chaos of the files I wrote of earlier. And now, some years after the first edition was released in Spain, comes the comment to comb it once more before it leaves my house again.

The Lighthouse was born in 2004, right after finishing *Hijos de la Alhambra. Hijos* was a tedious graphic novel to make: a lot of documentation, complicated perspectives, too much information to cram into few pages, coloring... My idea was to follow it up with the series *Los Viajes de Alexandre Ícaro* but before continuing with the next installment, I wanted to take a break and do something different, relaxed, a story that I could enjoy drawing.

PACO
ROCA 05

Illlustration of Francisco and Telmo done in 2005 (left) and sketches for the cover of the French edition (opposite page)

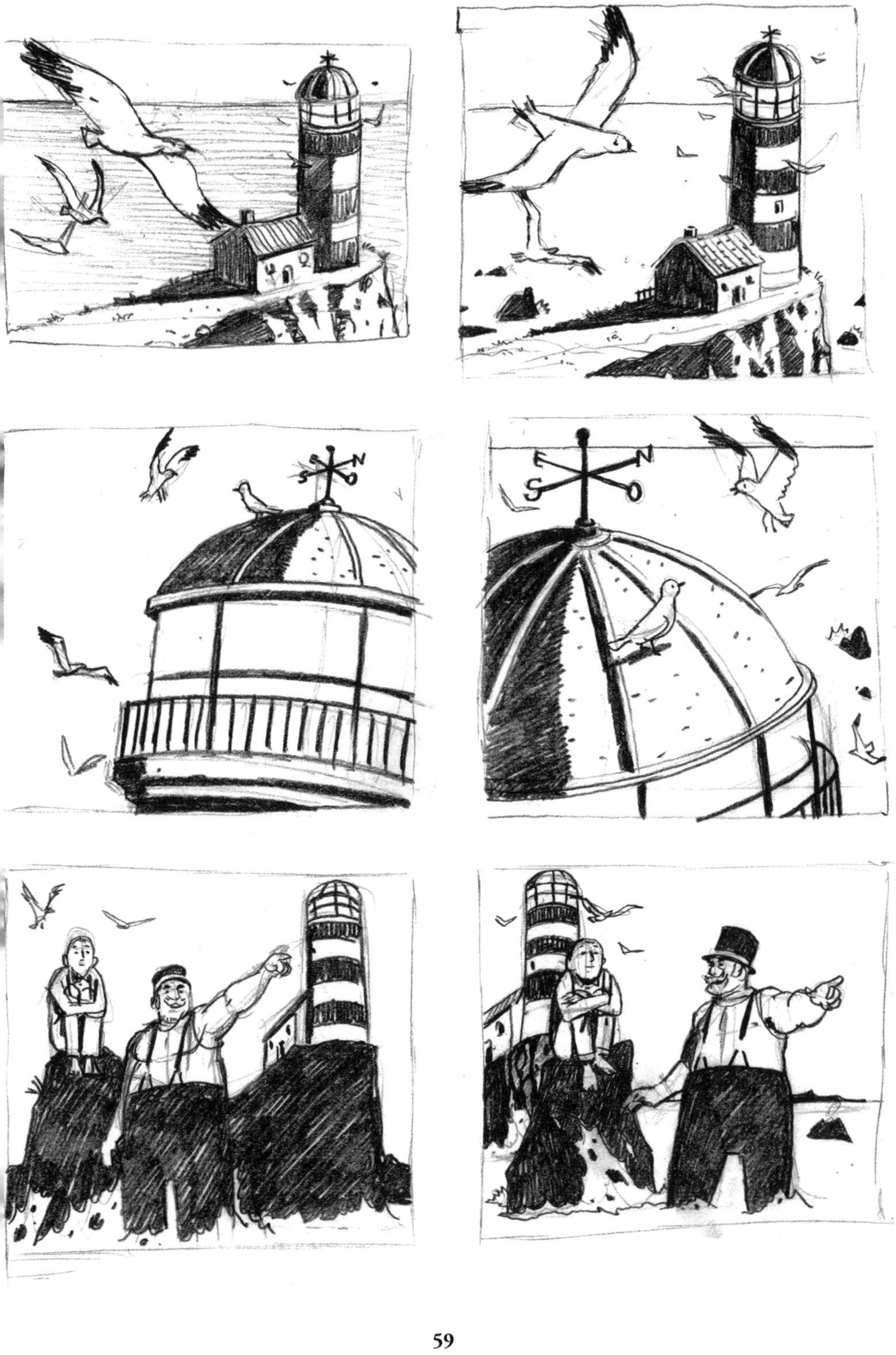
S N O
E N S O

I decided from the start that it would not be in color and the story must not need months of documentation before I could start working. I wanted something simple to be able to experiment with narration. I wanted to tell a relaxed story. Everything that I had done up until that moment had a very cinematic rhythm, the story would directly go to the resolution at an accelerated pace, without pause.

Photo of Francisco Valiente (above) and character designs for Francisco (below) and Telmo (opposite page)

I've always liked lighthouses so telling a story situated in one appealed to me. The starting point of the graphic novel is the Spanish Civil War, although it could be any other war. Francisco Valiente had fought in the Civil War and had told me many stories about the cruelty in those years, stories that practically all of us heard or read at one time or another, but what most interested me was his personal story. Francisco enlisted at sixteen in the riflemen and quickly after, when the war broke out, was sent to fight. He was in a losing brigade and escaped to France where he ended up together with the thousands of refugees in the humiliating concentration camp of Argeles. Upon the Civil War ending, he was returned to Spain only to be later sent to Morocco to do hard labor. For a long time, he could not return to his hometown in Almería and regain his life, stuck without hope or dreams. This loss of the will to live, so common in many of those defeated in the War, was what seemed interesting to me for *The Lighthouse*.

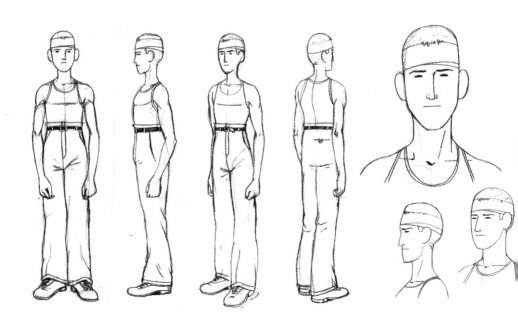

To begin my research in the maritime environment, I started to reread novels related to the sea that I read in my childhood: *The Lighthouse at the End of the World, Gulliver's Travels, Treasure Island*…movies like Jason and the Argonauts, Sinbad the Sailor…Once again I felt this "sensation of marvel" that I had felt as a small child. I thought that if all these stories had made me love adventure and formed part of my personality, they could also do that with the protagonist of *The Lighthouse* and return his will to live. And so *The Lighthouse* finally became a homage to all these stories of free men that sail the sea in search of adventure and a better world.

When I worked on the graphic novel, I remembered a text that I had read that perfectly defined what I was telling. The text talked about how an unfulfilled dream of one character was given to another for him to fulfill. I wanted to use it as the finale of the story, but I didn't know where I had read it. It has aspects of the stories of *A Thousand and One Nights*, but it was not among them. I asked around, I searched the internet, but I had no luck. In the end I decided to tell it as I remembered it. With time, and thanks to a conversation with Pepo Pérez, I discovered that the text was called *Historia de Los dos que Soñaron ("The Story of the Two Dreamers")*, and it's by Borges. This was inspired by a story in *A Thousand and One Nights*, the same one also used as inspiration by Coelho for *The Alchemist*.

So, one of the first doubts in putting together this new edition was if I should put that Borges text intact in the final pages. I ultimately decided to leave it as it is, changing just one small detail and adding a new interpretation of Borges's version of the original story from *A Thousand and One Nights*.

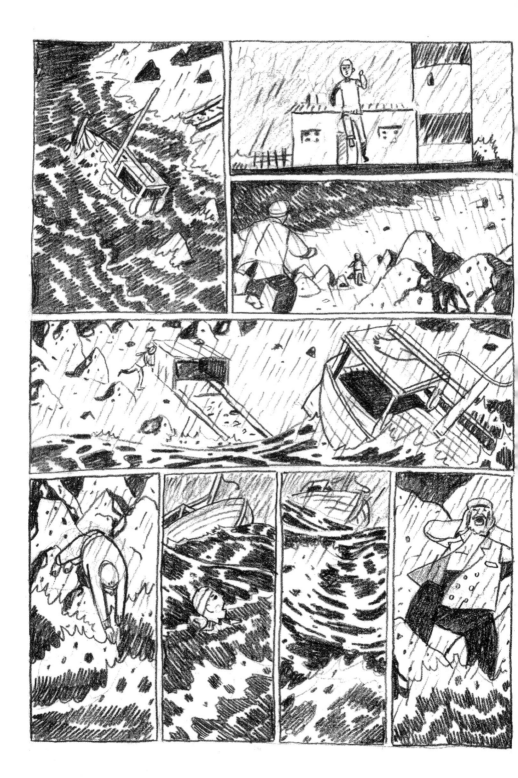

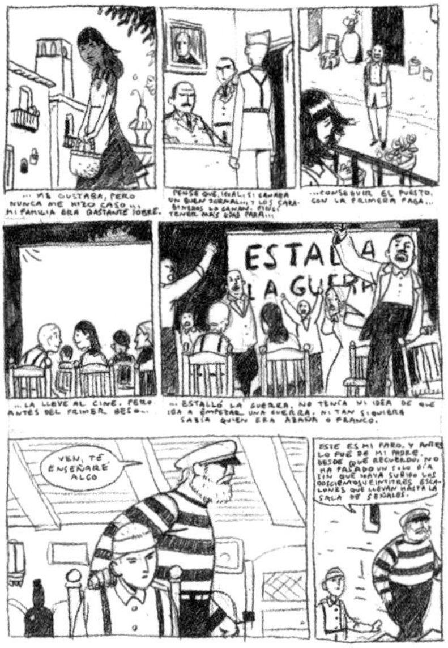
...ME GUSTABA, PERO NUNCA ME HIZO CASO... MI FAMILIA ERA BASTANTE POBRE.
...CONSEGUIR EL PUESTO. CON LA PRIMERA PAGA...
...LA LLEVÉ AL CINE. PERO ANTES DEL PRIMER BESO...
ESTAL A LA GU
...ESTALLÓ LA GUERRA. NO TENÍA NI IDEA DE QUE IBA A EMPEZAR UNA GUERRA. NI TAN SIQUIERA SABÍA QUIEN ERA AZAÑA O FRANCO.
VEN, TE ENSEÑARÉ ALGO
ESTE ES MI FARO. Y ANTES LO FUE DE MI PADRE.

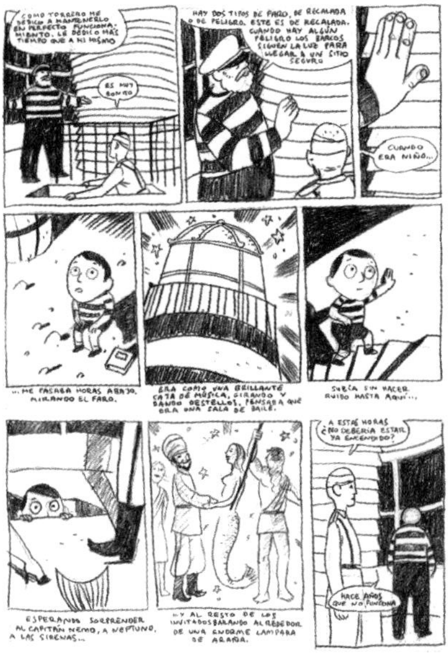
ES MUY BONITO
CUANDO ERA NIÑO...
...ME PASABA HORAS ABAJO, MIRANDO EL FARO.
SUBÍA SIN HACER RUIDO HASTA AQUÍ...
A ESTAS HORAS ¿NO DEBERÍA ESTAR YA ENCENDIDO?
HACE AÑOS QUE NO FUNCIONA
...Y AL RESTO DE LOS INVITADOS BAILANDO ALREDEDOR DE UNA ENORME LÁMPARA DE ARAÑA.

Pencil and ink sketches (opposite page and above) and the ad from TRAMA magazine (following page)

Apart from this necessary clarification, for this edition I was set from the beginning on lengthening the story, to add another scene, but I did not. I promptly realized that *The Lighthouse* is a tale and adding to it and lengthening it could break this structure, possibly even spoil it. We all would like to rewrite our past, re-do it more in line with who we are today, but this is a difficult and endless path. Looking at it again, *Las Calles de Arena* already is an updated and amplified version of *The Lighthouse*.

This is why in the end, the changes for this edition have been more subtle: rewriting some dialogue, retouching some panels, changing the cover page, adding a double page of the sea with the Melville quote to place us in this tranquil atmosphere of the story. Not to mention the great prologue by lighthouse keeper Enrique Luzuriaga.

So it is, with all this, *The Lighthouse* has left the house combed and I will wait, comb in hand, if I have to do it again.

Paco Roca
October 2009

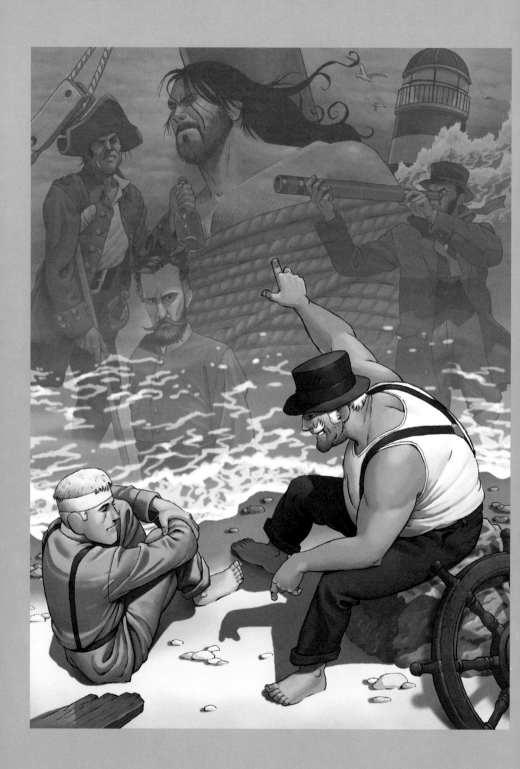

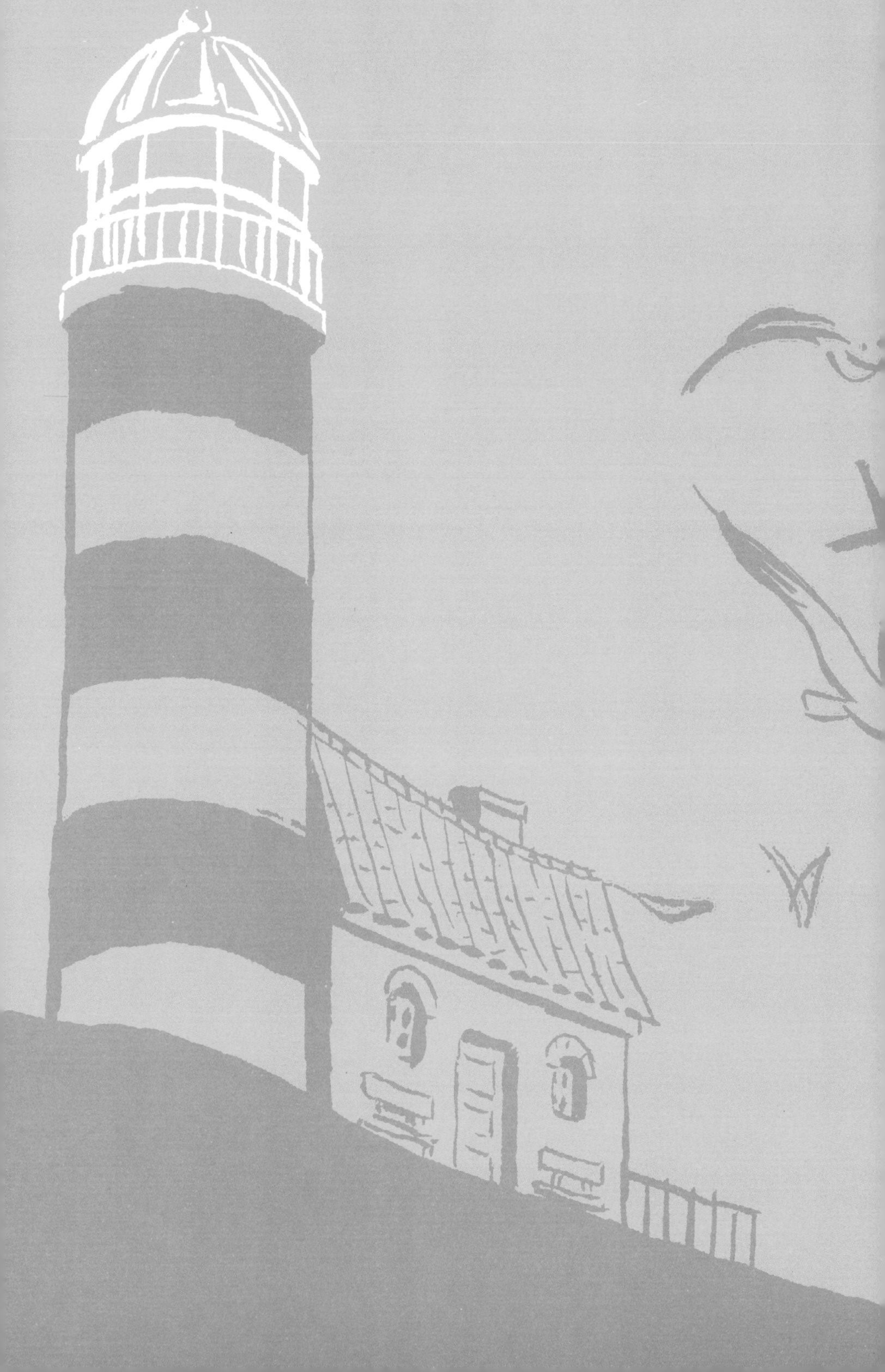